EXTRAORDINARY
TALES

FROM A
RATHER ORDINARY GUY

ED MARX

Published by Charles Pinot
Designed by Angela Conant

First Printing, 2014
10 9 8 7 6 5 4 3 2 1

Material in this book is for educational purposes only. This product is sold with the understanding that neither any of the authors nor the publisher are engaged in rendering legal, accounting, investment, or any other professional service specifically suited to one particular individual's needs who may be reading this book. Neither the publisher nor the authors assume any liability for any errors or omissions or for how this book or its contents are used or interpreted or for any consequences resulting directly or indirectly from the use of this book.

The views expressed by the individuals in this book do not necessarily reflect the views shared by the companies they are employed by (or the companies mentioned in this book). The employment status and affiliations of the authors with the companies referenced are subject to change.

I dedicate this book to my parents Herbert and Ida Marx.
They had nothing to give me but gave me everything,
Life. Love. Opportunity.

ACKNOWLEDGEMENTS

The stories in this book were made possible by people who believed in me before i believed in me. My parents Herbert and Ida Marx. They created the framework for my stories. My church pastors who guided me in my early adulthood and maturation of a man including Pastors, Rick Olmstead and Ric Lehman. All my bosses and mentors throughout the years who invested time and energy to shape me like best friends John Furste, Bruce Hallman, Jim Burton, Mary Hein, Mike Gogola and Kevin Roberts. My work cohorts who served tirelessly with me in Colorado, Tennessee, Ohio and Texas. Brandon and Talitha Marx, my kids who kept me humble along the way, teaching me all about technology! Most of all my beautiful bride of thirty years, Julie Marx."Like a lily among the thorns, so is my darling among the maidens." She has been the source of my passion. She took the potential and helped actualize it. Finally, my foundation on which I have received an unending supply of mercy and grace despite myself, my Creator.

TABLE OF CONTENTS

FOREWORD

Who is the real Edward Marx?

Next to God, only one person knows the down and dirty truth—the woman who shares his bed; who shakes her head at his best-foot-forward Facebook portrayal; who routinely confronts his toxic-smelling sports attire; and who competes with Miss Blackberry over marriage rights. Yes, I am Ed's wife, and I do not sugarcoat his life as he does. When he says, "The glass is half-full," I guzzle the contents and then hand the glass back to him. "How about now? Still half-full?"

Yes, Ed sprints through life with his sights set high and, admittedly, my realistic view of our temporal existence rarely makes him happy. But I'm not in this marriage to make Ed Marx happy. I'm here to point out the tripwires and snares in his path that he's too busy to see and, hopefully, push him back onto the narrow road toward what truly matters. It's a full-time job.

Having said all of that, I can more freely confess that I have borne witness to, if not participated in, ninety percent of the Extraordinary Tales in this book. Ed claims to be average, and he indeed is—with the exception of his extraordinary attitude. And his mindset is ever evolving. Back in college, Ed's desire to improve himself and his circle of influence was the one trait that most attracted me. When I evaluated the 18-year-old Army private in holey sweat pants and cheap cotton T-shirts, I caught a glimpse of a man with a sincere determination to become a better person all around, which would translate into better husband, better father, better employee, etc. I knew he would become someone amazing. Over the past 30 years—and despite his many character flaws—he has far exceeded my initial estimation.

At the core of his being, Ed Marx is a trailblazing leader and presenter. But this hasn't always been the case. I recall one day about 25 years ago. We were co-teaching a vision and mission workshop to a group of people at our church, and Ed began his portion by saying, "One caveat. I am not a public speaker...." After we concluded our workshop, Pastor Richard Powell walked up to him and with utmost seriousness declared, "Ed Marx, you are speaking in public, therefore you are a public speaker." Self-deception and self-deprecation gets us nowhere good.

Raising and promoting trendsetters stokes Ed's fire more than anything (except perhaps taking selfies while traveling so he can add "Scenes from an Early Morning Run" pictures to Facebook). I believe his heart's desire here is to tell tales that will help develop strong leaders, free readers to hone their imaginations, and inspire all to face their shortcomings and live boldly—because you get only one life to experience.

The world doesn't need another Edward Marx—trust me on this. What we do need are more innovators and fewer enervators. More creators and fewer critics. Greater imaginations and fewer imitations. As Lewis Carroll says, "If you don't know where you are going any road will get you there." So as you read these Extraordinary Tales, have your pen and pad...excuse me, your iPad and stylus handy for creating your personal strategic plan, complete with moral values to guide your choices. And then live mightily.

J.A. Marx

Multi-published author; fiction and non-fiction

PREFACE

"You are living my dream" is a common response I get when I meet people from around the world who have either read my blog or heard me speak. I never really know how to respond. I am all at once humbled—but frankly, I feel awkward. While I am thankful for the compliment, I feel sad for the person who is not living his dreams and instead lives vicariously through me or others. Most people I meet have accepted their lives as they are and have given up hope of achieving the extraordinary.

I come from humble beginnings and moreover, humbling genetics. I am not special. I am neither a Spartan or of superior intellect. In fact, like the majority of the people in the world I am, by definition, average. Perhaps slightly below average. I routinely received F's in junior high school. I was arrested twice in my teens. I lost all of my college financial aid after earning a 1.6 GPA. I was nearly booted out of Army basic training, and I got fired from my first career job. I never really dated. I am short. I eventually became bald. Despite all this, I continue to experience the extraordinary in my life. If I, being average, can live these extraordinary tales, then surely anyone can.

This internal dilemma forced me into introspection, searching for an answer as to why I have these extraordinary tales to share while so many people, especially those with superior intellect and resources, do not. What is the magic sauce? Is there a formula? I searched for years, reading books and listening to others promote their ideas, magic potions, even some snake oil. While many theories were touted, none hit home for me or resonated with my audiences. I came to the conclusion there really is no formula for success. For some it can be zeitgeist, and for others it's the silver spoon. But for everyday people like you and me, there is no magic pill or cookie cutter approach that will suddenly rocket us to the top of the world.

So, is there hope for those like you and me, the average?

As my extraordinary tales began to accumulate, I started making my own observations. During this process, I wondered if the rules I was living were influencing my personal and professional success and achievements. If there was a positive correlation, could they be repeated and replicated by others?

These maxims—the rules by which I try to live my life—are not my own creation, nor are they particularly revolutionary:

1. Risk boldly and often
2. Seek and chase vision
3. Believe in something bigger than you
4. Build a team of life givers
5. Embrace humility and service
6. Find and fuel passion
7. Perseverance and resiliency
8. Fail forward
9. Wonderment and continuous learning
10. Work your ass off
11. Volunteer and give until it hurts
12. Build strong identity
13. Physical fitness
14. Excellence

These fourteen rules each get a chapter in my book.

Over the years, I began teaching some of these life lessons to broad audiences across the globe. Although I did no scientific study, I did observe improvements in the lives of those who embraced these "ground rules" versus those who habitually followed the status quo. My discovery of these maxims did not come all at once—they did not arrive on stone tablets. As I discovered them and integrated them into my life, more extraordinary tales unfolded. Even I had to pinch myself a time or two to make sure I wasn't dreaming. As more of these tales and experiences unfolded, I felt compelled to tell other average people like me about the impact these rules had had on my life.

I am not promising instant success nor am I suggesting that this is a new and improved magic elixir that will lead to your own extraordinary tales. In fact, as you read through the table of contents and browse the chapters, you may find nothing new. The packaging may feel new, but overall, the maxims by which I am advocating that you aggressively adopt have been around since the beginning of time. If there is one difference, one secret to unlocking these extraordinary experiences, it is that I believe you must be "all in" with these rules. They do not come as part of our DNA. And while we might believe we live each of these every day, do we really? Are we fully immersed and creating opportunities? And that may be the difference. It is one thing to say you "embrace humility and service" or "work your ass off," but do you really?

Many people tell me they do "seek and chase vision." So I ask to hear their vision statement. I would guess that less than one percent of them have an articulate, well-thought-out vision for their life. While extraordinary tales can happen without a written statement, it is pretty hard to hit the bullseye when you can't describe the target. A well-defined target will help you fully immerse yourself and embrace these rules. Have you ever lost a job or responsibility because you "risked boldly and often?" If you have never suffered due to taking a risk, you have not fully embraced my approach.

If you are seeking to simply be entertained by stories, this book may or may not fulfill that need. These stories are written to inspire you to change. If you are looking for the beginnings of a road map to living your own extraordinary tales, read on.

Edward Marx

August 2014

1

RISK BOLDLY AND OFTEN

risk (risk), n.
1. exposure to the chance of injury or loss; a hazard or dangerous chance: *It's not worth the risk.*

For my generation, each day of growing up presented some new risk to take or some new challenge to meet. Whether it was a particularly high-branched tree begging to be climbed, finally facing down a bully at school who excelled at public humiliation, or lining up across from someone much bigger in that first tackle football game on a muddy field, most kids start off as fearless risk takers—and many end up with the bumps and bruises to prove it!

Somewhere in childhood we are shaped into playing life safe—we lose our propensity for risk-taking. Some of this learning is important and keeps us from losing life or limb, but more often than not, this healthy logic gets stretched far beyond any original intention. Over time this risk-averse, protective "bubble" can encompass much of our life. It happens slowly and unnoticeably but eventually it severely limits our potential to have extraordinary life experiences.

Everyone knows the saying, nothing ventured, nothing gained. The only way to have extraordinary experiences in life is to take risks.

I became a CIO when I was 35, most are 55 or older. In my case, the only reason I got the job was because I took a huge risk. Our CEO was leading the search for a CIO. He was a real tough guy, very intimidating. When someone would challenge him, he would stare at them until they backed down. I really thought I was qualified for the job, so I built up the courage to go to his office. I told him to stop the search—I was the guy for the job! I could hardly believe it, but he agreed and gave me the job. Later, he said that the reason he gave me the job was that I had the balls to stand up to him and go for it!

Risk boldly and often.

You have to take risks to reach the top in any aspect of your life. Whether it was getting up the nerve to ask my wife out when we first met (on a scale of 1-10, she's definitely a "9" and I am definitely a "5") or mountain climbing or competitive cycling, taking risks is the most important key to success. I talked with an Olympic cyclist and coach about leadership and the difference between cyclists who consistently finish "on the podium" and those who finish farther back in the pack. Both are great athletes—you have to be to compete at that level. She told me it's all about risk.

The best cyclists know that if they play it safe and stay in the peloton, they can finish in the top ten. The cyclists who break away from the pack and charge up a long hill are the risk takers. They know that if they are successful, they will usually be among the podium finishers. They also know that if something goes wrong—a blowout or accident while they are pushing that envelope as hard as they can, they might finish well down the list. The Olympic cycling coach told me that she always looks for those people—the ones willing to take risks. I do the same when I am looking for people to hire. A lot of people say they don't like to take risks, that they weigh the pros and cons and then make a conservative decision. Sometimes that is good, but if you are too conservative—in business or in racing—you will never make it to the top. When I hire, I want people who are willing to take risks for the right reasons.

Most people let fear rule their lives. I refuse to do that. I want not just the rewards that come from taking a risk, but also the experience. I thrive on the feeling I get when I am pushing the envelope. When I climb a mountain, I am scared to death and loving it.

Why live a life without risk?

THE unEXPERIENCED LIFE IS NOT WORTH LIVING

Socrates' famous phrase about "the unexamined life" has made its way into many lectures and speeches. It is advice known to many. I'm not a philosopher, but I researched Socrates and, I stumbled across a distinction he made between people (Athenians) who watched life and those who experienced it. Olympic athlete crossing the finish line displays a "semblance of success," but is it true reality? We love to admire superb performances and bask in a new world record. But what would happen if we personally strove for such experiences ourselves?

I choose to experience life. It doesn't need be extravagant or expensive. Life can be as simple as turning off the soccer match on TV and joining a local team, or signing up for a ballroom dance class rather than just watching "Dancing with the Stars." Instead of reading books about the missionaries in India, you can instead sign up to help at your local soup kitchen. You can step away from your Facebook account and instead host a get-together with people you know or would like to know.

Doing is better than spectating.

My original plan in writing this book was to share with you insights from a recent climb I made of Europe's highest mountain, Mount Elbrus. That was a victorious experience tempered by a tragedy that unfolded two days after the climb.

Tradition in the climbing world calls for celebration following a summit. While touring St. Petersburg, I was walking down the city's bustling Main Street with five members of my team. We were trading climbing stories and talking about what motivated us to climb. People we met along the way said interesting things about the danger of climbing mountains. Our response was, "Life is short, and a sheltered life was no life at all. You might get hit by a car while playing it safe, so you may as well embrace risk."

Although still light outside, midnight was approaching as we began the journey back to our hotel. Approaching the intersection by the Kazan Cathedral, we formed a quasi-column so we could pass pedestrians coming from the other side. I entered the crosswalk, leading my friends. We were immediately behind two ladies who looked to be in their twenties. Then, in a split second, tires screeched, headlights blazed, and I instinctively dove out of the way. To my left, I heard flesh hit metal…then glass breaking (a windshield). As I landed on the ground, from the corner of my eye I saw the two women cartwheeling through the air. By the time I rolled to a stop, they had landed ten meters away. Unconscious. Contorted. Broken. A surreal scene.

After a few seconds to express our rage and gather our wits about us, we jumped into action. JJ, our mountain guide, took command. We became doctors, EMTs and comforters. We stabilized both of the women. A dozen policemen showed up but then stood around completely clueless, staring at us. I have a vivid recollection of my bunkmate Frank clasping one woman's hand and speaking calmly to her. She told us she was visiting from Siberia. Her friend lay unconscious with her head held stable by our buddy Zac. At the ten-minute mark, a "first aid" vehicle showed up, and a woman wearing scrubs emerged. But she was with infection control and had no actual medical supplies. Limited to applying smelling salts, she was trying to get both women up and walking without having assessed the severity of their injuries.

Adding to the chaos, a policeman grabbed Zac, thinking he was the negligent driver, and tried to arrest him. Bystanders intervened, and Zac was released. We continued providing support to the women, but our counsel to the "infection lady" and the swarming, interfering bystanders was ignored. Ms. Infection Control was forcing the second patient, now conscious, to move despite obvious skeletal trauma. I backed off and prayed over the situation, asking God to send the Holy Spirit for comfort, healing and wisdom. Not having our passports in hand, we left a few minutes later as the mob grew more aggressive. My team prayed from a distance.

Back in the hotel room, I buried my head in a bath towel and sobbed. I Skyped my wife. Every time I closed my eyes, I saw those ladies doing cartwheels over me. I slept for three hours and then returned to the scene, which had since been cleared. I wondered what had happened to the two Siberian women and how they were doing. Who was looking over them? Who was holding their hands? Were they still alive? I spent another thirty minutes simply praying and reflecting on the evening's events. I could not stop crying.

To this day, my team is still processing what we experienced. As traumatic as it was, we were glad we'd been there and hoped the aid we provided had helped to save a life. We witnessed first-hand how quickly life can be taken away in a blink of an eye by while doing something as innocuous as crossing a street.

Life is filled with tragedy and heartbreak. You can bank on it. But does adversity really hold us back? I'd venture to say it's our fear-based beliefs gleaned from painful incidences or even simply the possibility of tragedy that paralyzes us. Instead of falling prey to paralysis, when we experience the depth of heartbreak we grow stronger from it. Conquer the fear and keep living.

Living life with no regrets means requires us to crawl out of the ashes of tragedy and walk away stronger. With purpose.

Determine to live a life fully experienced. We live.

IT'S NOT ABOUT THE ROCK
(THE REMOTE VILLAGE THAT TURNED OUR LIVES UPSIDE DOWN)

"Ed," Dr. Liz Ransom whispered in my ear, "why aren't we doing a medical mission? After all, we're mostly a bunch of docs."

I nodded my agreement. Her point was obvious and I announced the change that same meeting. Instead of a purely educational mission, we would set up a medical clinic. And so, approximately nine months before our departure to Tanzania to climb Mount Kilimanjaro, our idea for a modest medical clinic was conceived.

We leveraged important connections thanks to another friend and company board member, Jimmy Wynne. In fact, Jimmy was the one who suggested climbing Kilimanjaro. Thanks to previous personal investments he had made in this remote Maasai village of 10,000, he knew the local government officials as well as the tribal elders. These relationships were key to our proposed clinic's success and long-term viability.

Our team members pooled resources. One thing led to another, and our plans for the clinic grew from a tent to a more permanent structure. Before we broke ground, our friends, Doug and Martha Hawthorne, got involved and enlarged our vision. They donated the additional funds needed to create a larger structure that would eventually be equipped with running water and electricity. Blueprints were redrawn and weeks later we received a letter from the government pledging their long-term support of the clinic after we left. Sustainability was a non-negotiable issue for us; with that objective met, dirt began to move.

While we were busy preparing for our climb, construction of the upcoming "Open Arms Clinic" continued. Onsite contacts sent periodic updates with pictures, so we could manage the project from afar. Another friend of ours and a hospital president, Winjie Tang Miao, agreed to act as the clinic director, with Liz Ransom serving as the medical director. Winjie and Liz worked closely to handle all of the clinic details: inventory, staffing, medical recordkeeping, workflow, etc.

In June 2011, we arrived in Arusha, Tanzania. While the climbing team left for seven days to tackle Kilimanjaro, five women from our party traveled four hours by bus in the opposite direction to a remote village near Mto wa Mbu. Their trip did not start well. Our male American liaison, with whom we had been coordinating for months, missed the introductory meeting with the village elders. That first night our group of five women (including my wife and daughter) sat alone across the table from fifteen Maasai village elder warriors armed with spears. Despite having two awesome translators (one for Swahili, a second for Maa), the talks were very awkward. The Maasai are a chauvinist culture, yet the discussions about the clinic involved information regarding safe sex and AIDS. This curious conversation would either result in a mutually trusting relationship or create a major obstacle to the clinic's successful operation.

So while the majority of us climbed Kilimanjaro, the real superstars—our five-woman team at the village—succeeded in making introductions, finalizing plans and helping to educate the villagers. My then 17-year-old daughter Talitha proved to be the critical bridge between the villagers and our team. When the Maasai elders realized we could teach them the basics of wellness: nutrition, health and universal precautions, they embraced the opportunity.

By the time the rest of us climbed Mt. Kilamanjaro and arrived at the village, clinic construction was almost completed, but still a few days behind. It would open without water or electricity.

June 22 was opening day for the Open Arms Clinic. Seventeen of the twenty local Representatives from the Tanazanian Assembly plus a former Prime Minister attended the incredible ribbon-cutting celebration. Doug and Martha Hawthorne represented our team and together with the Prime Minister blessed the clinic. Villagers dressed in a vast array of colors, surrounding their new clinic and singing in Maa. This put most of our team in tears; I hid mine behind a camera lens. We were all humbled and a little awed by the fanfare as we saw how much the clinic meant to the Maasai and their country. Media from all over Tanzania had their cameras rolling. A major party wrapped up the opening day events.

The following morning we opened for business. Winjie and Liz had everything well organized. We had a doctor and medical assistant for each of the four treatment rooms plus another team working in the lobby. The triage unit included two assistants and two translators. They prepared the clinic's first medical records, took vitals, and prioritized patients. Two women staffing the supply room/pharmacy/break room dispensed medicines and supplies. The rest of our team rotated between crowd control and entertaining all the kids. We played lots of soccer and taught the Maasai children American style football and Frisbee.

Our first patient was a young mother who had not felt her baby move in over 36 hours. "Oh great," I heard myself saying, "what if our first two patients die?" What would be the risk to the clinic longevity? Would the villagers turn hostile? Had we lured all these people here to die? Even if the village accepted such deaths as inevitable, the loss of our first patients would cast a dour vibe over the clinic. What an ominous beginning! I prayed but, as much as I hate to admit it, my thoughts were more negative than positive.

While I was growing more and more uptight, our medical team swung into action. Scott Ransom, one of our doctors was an OB/GYN. Liz Ransom, our medical director and Scott's spouse, also went with our first patient into the "birthing suite." She held the mother's hand and assisted her husband with the delivery. Given their different specialties, this was the first time Liz and Scott had ever practiced together.

Outside, it seemed the entire village had gathered as news spread quickly (without Facebook). Crowds pressed in and my thoughts grew darker as we held the line. I could hear the rest of the team behind me going in and out of the room, but no cries from a newborn baby. Someone shouted for one of the other doctors, Doug [LASTNAME?], who by "coincidence" happened to be a neonatologist. When he entered the room, I figured the baby had been born. Unbeknownst to me, Doug, his wife, and some of our ladies were meeting in the pharmacy room to hold hands and pray.

Silence fueled my anxiety. The eager crowd grew antsy. Some had traveled many miles to receive treatment and this incident held things up.

Resuscitation attempts were underway. Lacking the requisite equipment, improvisation came into play. A plastic baggie turned into an ambu bag (a manual resuscitator), a shoelace became a clamp. Ten minutes passed, then the baby took a breath on her own. The precious infant pinked up, and then… a cry that brought hope. Those in the birthing room heaved a deep sigh and then came the tears. That one cry carried a message to all the villagers *and* (as we found out later) reached the Serengeti, a four-hour drive away.

The message: Open Arms Clinic is a good place!

Isina (the mother) suffered a second-degree tear. The only suture available was a 5-0 chromic suture, but we had no needle driver. The OB/GYN found makeshift suture scissors and sewed up the tear. All this time Liz had been consoling the mother, Isina, and serving as her birthing coach. Liz built a bond with the first-time mother. Toward the end, Isina asked her name, and our Medical Director replied, "Elizabeth Ransom." While the physicians continued their work, Isina announced, "I am naming my baby Elizabeth."

Everyone in the room began to cry. Nine months earlier, Elizabeth Ransom had been the person who suggested we set up a clinic. Coincidence?

The Open Arms Clinic continues to serve this remote village to this day. An African physician and nurse now run the day-to-day operation. The government continues to honor its commitment of service. Several original team members continue to provide in-kind support. Teams still return for visits. In just the first week we provided care to 350+ patients and witnessed still more miracles.

Our group did not have to open a clinic in that village. Many would have thought that our climb up Kilimanjaro was plenty of risk to take. We could have just settled for the educational trip. We did not. We took bold risks and reaped incredible rewards.

We went to climb a mountain but found our trip wasn't about Kilimanjaro. While we impacted a village of 10,000 in a remote part of the world, that village turned our own world upside down. We came back changed, transformed, as the villagers were. We grew as leaders. As friends. As individuals. We found ourselves. We deepened our faith. Our lives will never be the same.

It's not about the rock.

INNOVATION IS LEADERSHIP

After thirty years of putting it off, I finally did it. I got braces. Yes, the shiny, stainless steel that is the bane of fragile teenage egos. Braces represent risk-taking at its highest and most visible level, whether the risk taker is a fragile teenager or a mature, confident adult.

Sadly, the technology related to braces has not changed. Take, for instance, the cosmic, Michael Strahan-like gap between my two front teeth. The dentist glued the brackets to my teeth and pulled wire through them. On repeat visits he will tighten them—a slow torture that will span almost three years. After recent painful, nanometer adjustments, I lamented that this technology has experienced little innovation over the past fifty years. While there are magical products to make the appliance less visible, nothing has actually evolved by way of clinical efficacy—a sizeable gap I liken to the one between my teeth.

"Best practices" are a regression to the mean —wouldn't you agree? Our love affair with the term "best practices" is really another way of embracing the *average*. We are desperate for improved and enhanced ways of doing things yet the best most of us can manage is to copy someone else—a collective slide into mediocrity.

Innovate—take a risk—or perish.

Plenty of scholarly evidence substantiates my critique. You cannot pick up any kind of business literature without reading about the dearth of innovation in the United States. Healthcare is as fertile a ground for a much needed influx of innovation as any other vertical market. Innovation takes on many forms from technical to transactional to cultural. Most readers should already be familiar with Clayton M. Christensen's works, *The Innovator's Dilemma* and *The Innovator's Solution*. More recently, Christensen applied his innovation concepts to healthcare with a landmark piece, *The Innovators Prescription*, a mandatory read for any healthcare leader.

What can you and I do to spark innovation in healthcare and in our organizations? First, we start with our own lives, and second, our span of control.

Career mimics persona. If you are innovative, it will reflect in everything you do—work, play, relationships, etc. To remain or become innovative, you must embrace a lifestyle that matches your career path. I don't mean the old pat-on-the-back hug, but an embrace of lovers reunited. Do you select hobbies that require creativity and imagination?

One reason I've immersed myself in the Argentine Tango is because there are no right or wrong moves. Instead, I can take the 2-4 count patterns I've learned and arrange them according to the feel of the music or mood. What this means is that I have to think afresh for every song yet maneuver in a way that allows my partner space to be equally artistic.

The triathlon, another of my passions, is credited for inspiring transformational improvements in cycling, sports clothing, and sporting accessories that other sports have adopted. As a sport, the triathlon itself continues to evolve.

As hobbies, dancing and competing in triathlons work for me. Clearly, these choices may not work for you. There are thousands of choices that can speak to your personality and ambitions. The point is to pick something that stretches you. If I ever grow comfortable, I'll know I've become stagnant. And my career will imitate my life.

At work, you must be boldly intentional. While I do a fair amount of speaking on a variety of leadership-related topics, the most common request I receive is to speak on innovation. After giving the keynote at a recent Computerworld Conference, the audience enthusiastically embraced innovation. It doesn't just happen. You have to promote innovation with sound processes to woo the un-initiated. You can create innovation portals that showcase processes and how to get involved, set up reward systems as encouragement, or even hold contests where all submissions have to be done via video, a creative process in itself. Re-cruit judges from your C-suite to ensure high visibility.

The truly ambitious might want to host a TEDx event, a new program that enables local communities such as schools, businesses, libraries, neighborhoods or just groups of friends to organize, design and host their own independent TED-like events. Or pick a technology that you think has potential and invite a wide variety of participants to help brainstorm innovation. Such a mash-up could lead to some amazing outcomes that, for example, could transform clini-cal care. The most pioneering ideas will come from people who are closest to the action and who are waiting for a forum to speak out. An innovative leader acts as a catalyst and creates an environment suitable for originality.

No single idea will transform a staid business culture into one of innova-tion. Nevertheless, as you begin to mix in such ideas, processes, and events, you will have an impact, and a subculture of transformation will begin to take hold. Anticipate resistance and accept it as positive feedback. If you don't encounter resistance, *redouble your efforts.*

Live in such a way that no one will ever look back at your career or your life and say, "not much changed." Like the battle between my teeth and stainless steel, change may not be noticeable on a day-to-day basis, but over time incre-mental change becomes transformative

LEGACY LEADERS

How can so many of us hold the title of leader, yet so few of us be remem-bered? Why do some "leaders" make a difference while others do not? I can answer that in one word: Fear.

Fear keeps us from making a difference. Too often leaders fade without notice or just the slightest modicum of fanfare despite their longevity in a company. Why? Because they stayed the course, stuck with tradition, and their wins were small and inconsequential. Conversely, legacy leaders stick their necks out, occasionally going against the flow. They spin the roulette wheel while their peers play it safe. Anyone can play safe—status quo. But legacy leaders fight their fears, calculate their options and then jump in with both feet.

Leaders who leave legacies take risks.

No risk, no legacy. Our Founding Fathers pursued a risky mission, but look at the legacy they left us. Martin Luther King, Jr., took risks that prematurely ended his life, but his legacy endures. Pause for a moment and try to think of a leader praised by history whose fame is based entirely on competent administration. Good luck coming up with one.

I overhear leaders say they want to make a difference, that they want to transform healthcare locally and nationally. Yet most healthcare is stuck in neutral, if not *reverse*. Decision makers are overly conservative in their approach to innovation and opportunity. Paradoxically, some I know in management were risk takers early in their careers, enjoyed success and were promoted. For whatever reason, they then shifted gears and assumed a risk-averse posture before running out of gas well short of their destination. We as healthcare leaders must intrepidly drive forward, or surrender the wheel to someone who will.

If we want to encourage and reward the courageous, the best way is to lead by example. Push the envelope. Try new programs, systems, and services before they're mainstreamed. Never settle for lip service, fund and staff risky ventures. Then reward risk takers publicly, even when they fail, *because they gave it their all*. Perseverance will eventually pay off.

Risk provides a competitive advantage. Do you want to create separation and differentiation in your marketplace? Take risks. Tap into the creativity of those employees with a passion to innovate and transform. Yes, there will be some failures. Use those failures as a vaccine to increase your risk tolerance.

Don't learn the wrong lesson and shy away from risk. Learn to accept and embrace failure, and then learn from it. Thomas Edison did.

Avoid analysis paralysis. Adopt Colin Powell's Leadership Lesson #15, "P = 40 to 70." P stands for the probability of success; the numbers indicate the percentage of information acquired. Once the information is in the 40 to 70 range, go with your gut. Procrastination in the name of reducing risk actually increases the potential of failure or falling behind.

To those who still favor a conservative approach to their business, I ask, "do you fear losing your job?" When you play safe, your reward is keeping your position, right? But if you don't rock the boat or challenge the status quo, don't you inevitably lose part of your soul?

A board vice chair once told me, "Ed, if you do your job right, you won't be here a year from now." I took his comment as encouragement to take risks on behalf of our patients and providers. If I lost my job in the process, so be it. I did not operate out of fear of my boss but from my fear of *not* influencing my part of the business.

Risk is a lifestyle, not just a work mode. When hiring like-minded staff, determine the risk quotient of potential candidates by finding out what they do outside of work. If they stick to the standard fare, move on. If they play it safe, move on. They won't act any different in the workplace.

What about you? Are you a legacy leader making a difference? Will anyone remember your years of effort? Will healthcare be transformed because of your actions?

What are you doing today that is risky? What are you doing today to encourage risk?

Demand it. Live it.

TRADITION!

I love Broadway. One benefit of having worked in Cleveland for eight years was our proximity to the crown of the city, Playhouse Square. Playhouse represented the largest U.S. theatre district outside of Broadway. We enjoyed the most famous shows as well as the emerging ones and even added our then pre-teen children as subscribers to offer them a taste of culture. Broadway struck me as remarkable considering my youthful idea of entertainment had been rumbling in a mosh pit back in the day slamming to the Boomtown Rats, Missing Persons, and The Clash, to name a few.

Our first show was *Fiddler on the Roof*, the marvelously deep story of Tevye, father of five daughters. Tevye struggled to maintain balance when outside influences encroached upon his religious traditions and his family. His three eldest daughters inched aggressively toward abandoning the established customs of a Jewish marriage by choosing their own husbands, forcing Tevye to question their age-old practices. Meanwhile, the Tsar was working to evict the Jews from Anatevka, their village. Tevye had to decide whether to stay and die fighting, or move on. He lived a precarious existence, like that of a fiddler on a roof. He lived between the future and…Tradition!

His story connected with the fiddler in me, for I also lived in the tense place between old and new, tradition and innovation, the good old days and the brave new world. When my family journeyed to the United States from Germany in 1975, we preserved our Bavarian traditions. I wore *lederhosen* to school, and it didn't take long to see that I was not up to date with Western culture. It took a while but I finally convinced my boss—*I mean my Mother*—to buy me a pair of blue jeans. Mom's sauerbraten and spätzle, on the other hand, I'll never give up!

Thanks to the experiences of my youth, I keep abreast of trends, culturally and in business. Desiring to thrive in my work rather than just survive, I lean progressively towards the new and bold. At times it can be frightening to step into unexplored or unconventional territory. But the benefit is worth the risk. Imperfect and painful? Oh yes, but better to endure the fiery path of innovation than to languish beneath the yoke of tradition.

Sit back for a moment and assess your life. Now assess your workplace. Are you where you should be, or are you wearing lederhosen to work?

"But it's my organization that lives in the obsolete world, not I," you say.

Yes, organizations are full of traditions and each has its own fiddler on the roof. Some traditions are important, yet many endure simply because of ... Tradition! Tradition for tradition's sake is inevitably exposed when groundbreaking ideas are presented, especially those introduced by individuals new to the organization. I pity the organization whose culture is steeped so deeply in tradition that attempts to introduce innovations and foreign concepts are summarily rebuffed, leaving that organization to smother, unchanged. Unfortunately, those passionate leaders who could help advance an organization into the latest fashion (i.e., blue jeans) could get discouraged and leave. Or worse, they'll allow themselves to be assimilated, acquiescing to tradition.

In this day and age, technology is progressing at such a rapid pace that an IT leader cannot be timid in exploiting it. Do you want to make a difference or not? Do you remember why you got into this business? Are you staying true to that calling? Or have you been beaten down over the years by those who refuse to innovate? For some of you, it's time to resurrect the vision that once inspired you to exuberantly seek to change the healthcare world, to have a positive impact on patient safety and the quality of care.

As an industry, we've got to care enough to not let ourselves become complacent. Whether or not you're new to your organization, shake the bonds of tradition-for-tradition's-sake and lead boldly. Just like Tevye's daughters (Tzeitel, Hodel, Chava) you also must push forward. We can all learn from Hodel's suitor Perchik who, tired of rhetoric and feel-good culture, chooses to blaze a new trail.

Will blazing a new trail lead you to danger? Will it possibly put your position at risk? Probably. But aren't the advancements we fight for worth the risk? Shouldn't we crusade to bring about prosperity for our patients and employers? These are risks I gladly embrace.

I'd rather choose progress than wither under...TRADITION!

FACING FEAR: A KEY PERFORMANCE INDICATOR

I was on the bottom of the ocean, staring up at the surface. One moment I had been standing on the beach, in the next I was carried out into a watery abyss by the rip tide. I paddled up toward the light and broke through, gasping for breath.

Spring Break of 1988 began well. My wife and I had free tickets to Kauai to visit my in-laws to introduce them to our baby boy. During our son's cuddle time with his grandparents, my wife and I made our way down Kauai's north shore, the Na Pali Coast, to get a closer look at the magnificent Pacific. We took took some pictures before heading back up the lone path. I stood at the edge of a rocky outcropping several meters above the ocean surf. I smiled, said "cheese." A second later, we were both knocked down by the wave that took me out to sea.

Bloody knees, winter surf, rocky shoreline—I was still clearly in danger. Swimming parallel to the shore while outmaneuvering the breakers was not easy; the pummeling waves and the force of the undertow sapped my energy. I was scared. Gradually working my way closer to shore, I prayed the waves would not crush me against the wall of boulders lining the island. Three or four people meet death that way every winter on Kauai. After much prayer, my feet touched solid ground. I quickly scrambled up the cliff before the tide could reclaim me.

Despite being an active triathlete, I've purposefully avoided the ocean. I've tackled lakes and rivers, but never the open sea. After my experience on Kauai, even though it was long ago, I'm still afraid. Recently an opportunity opened up for me to race in one of the triathlon's foremost events, *Escape from Alcatraz*. My fear of the ocean consumed me and I considered passing on the competition as too risky! But instead I said yes, determined to swim across the San Francisco Bay, avoiding sharks and undertows alike.

I knew that if I didn't face my fear, it would own me.

Once I feared public speaking, as well. Now I love it. Despite the now familiar butterflies before each engagement, I press on. To further practice and hone my speaking skills, I now seek out speaking opportunities.

I also once feared challenging business peers —respectfully, of course. After I overcame that, I went on to conquer my fear of challenging my managers. Iron sharpens iron, as they say. We experience growth by pushing each other as we move forward toward a greater purpose.

Many who feel "stuck" in their careers are likely limiting themselves out of fear. Are you afraid to rock the boat? Are you afraid to take a risk? Do you comply dutifully with every request even though you may know a better way? One way to accelerate your career is to continually pursue growth. The second way is to embrace a willingness to combat fears, not letting them own you.

Do you fear being fired for speaking up? What about the chance of being wrong or laughed at? I've been there. Others fear success and the additional performance expectations that come with it. I say, embrace your fears. Confront them. Then you can experience freedom.

One of my present fears is dancing an entire song with our Argentine Tango instructor. I can handle learning an individual move, but the pressure of a performing a complete dance with an expert just kills me. I sweat. I forget how to speak. I even forget the move we just learned. But I'm smart enough to understand that unless I tackle this fear head on, my skills will not grow. And that is unacceptable. I won't tolerate complacency. You shouldn't either.

Reflect and write down your fears. Be brutally honest with yourself. Then attack your fears one-by-one, and with purpose. Take the risk. You will be amazed at the results. And I'll bet you will find that you are not alone. Not only will you grow, but so will your family and employer.

Growth inspires others to grow.

2
SEEK AND CHASE VISION

vis • ion (vizh'ən), n.
1. the act or power of sensing with the eyes; sight. 2. the act or power or anticipating that which will or may come to be: prophetic vision.

A proverb suggests that without vision, people wander.

Most people are unable to answer the simple question, "what is your vision?" Neither can they answer, "what is your purpose?" Many people will devote more time to figuring out their lucky lottery numbers than they will on the critical questions of why they exist, what they are here to accomplish.

Extraordinary experiences are rooted in vision. If you do not live with intention, you will never live your dreams.

You have to be very purposeful about what you want to accomplish. A lot of people get tossed around by the waves of life and when they grow older they ask themselves why they did not accomplish all that they wanted to.

People do not have a sense of where they want to go and so they wander through their entire lives. If you have dreams, the only way to live them is to have the vision to attain them and then take steps to make them happen.

"Vision without execution is a broken promise." Most of us do not believe that we have what it takes to achieve our vision. We live in constant self doubt. Yet steadfastly pursuing your vision can make you do extraordinary things.

One of my dreams is to climb the highest peak on every continent (except for Everest). I have envisioned myself doing this, and am accomplishing the goal I have set for myself.

Throughout my life I have been a classic example of the average person. But when I am empowered by a vision and driven by passion, I can be absolutely extraordinary. This is not specific to me, anyone can do this!

What Do I Stand For?
But I still wake up . . .
Oh Lord, I'm still not sure, what I stand for
What do I stand for? Oh what do I stand for?
Most nights, I don't know anymore

I like the tune *Some Nights* by the indie alternative group *fun*. You can argue the meaning of the song or whether to capitalize the name of the band (they don't), but the hook, *what do I stand for?* resonates with millions of people, myself included. The one issue people struggle with most is discovering their purpose in life and developing a vision based on that purpose. I'm frequently invited to speak on this, and it is a concern about which people often ask my help.

I have no secret formula nor can I warrant that what worked for me and my family will work for you. Making life easy and eliminating challenge is not my goal. Finding one's purpose inherently involves trials. What I can offer are guiding principles and a process for facilitating your journey into discovery, one that could potentially transform your life on multiple levels. For years I've shared these ideas with people from different cultures and always have witnessed dramatic change result when these principles and process are embraced.

When asked for help the first thing I ask is, "What's your plan?" That's a big, general question that encompasses your mission, vision, values, objectives, etc. I've never received an *articulate* first-time response. But when I ask people about their organization's plan, they are quick to answer.

The dichotomy is evident. Why would you invest your time memorizing and laboring to achieve the plans of your organization, but not do the same for yourself or your family? The good news is that you already possess the tools and experience to do this. It takes time, energy, and determination, and you must believe it's important or it will not get done.

I finished graduate school in 1989 with business planning concepts drilled into my brain. My company embraced these concepts, and I watched as our executives jetted off to resorts to spend considerable amounts of time planning. Market performance confirmed a strong correlation. But for me, I saw a disconnect when the same executives would recount their struggles on the personal side of their life's ledger. One particular article in *Fortune* magazine article reinforced my thought process: "Why Grade 'A' Execs Get an 'F' as Parents." The title spoke to me.

I had just started a family and a career; I was searching for ways to succeed in both. After reading the article in Fortune I asked myself, *could I increase the odds of success by adopting business theory in my personal life?*

I decided that it couldn't hurt to try!

The Marx family's strategic planning and vision adventure began modestly. Short, inexpensive trips away from home reduced distractions and stimulated creativity. Our trips morphed into more elaborate excursions, but the focus always remained on strategic planning. Our first retreat in nearby Estes Park, Colorado, cost us about $100. We worked on a one-page plan that became known as the "Marx Family Constitution." Originally written in 1990, it has withstood the test of time.

Since incorporating this process, everyone in my family has experienced dramatic increases in the quality of our respective careers and relationships. Our oldest, now 26, coached his college peers in these concepts. Not long ago, my wife heard our youngest, now 19, encourage her boyfriend to discover his life purpose and come up with a plan to live it out. My wife Julie and I recently celebrated our 29th wedding anniversary and are still, as young people say, twitterpated with each other as we continue to live out the vision we had for our lives together

I don't have the space to share every example, but I will share one that had the most impact on us. My son, age eight at the time, took a ruler and pointed to the values section of our Marx Family Constitution that hung prominently in our family room. "Dad," he said, "was that honoring mom when you yelled?" Seven months prior, when deciding which six values needed improvement, he had contributed the word "honor." He called me on it and by holding me accountable, he reinforced the value of our Marx Family Constitution to all of us.

We aim to live out what Rick Warren calls "The Purpose Driven Life." Decisions on how to spend our time, energy, and resources are guided by past family retreats. I could go back through twenty years of documentation and show you at least one significant event that happened each year of my career, marriage, and family. Can you say the same?

Annual retreats allow you to focus on your plan. Get out of Dodge and spend time in a setting where beauty can inspire you. If you are your family's leader, your job is to facilitate. WARNING: never force your ideas down your family's throats. Instead, invite them to dream and evaluate. Kids especially need to think for themselves. Review your plan and encourage transparent dialogue about performance. Record the highlights of the previous year (I told you up above that I had documentation). What are the gaps between plan and highlights, and how do you close them? Include significant others in your retreats and engage your kids. Teach them. Envision their success but NEVER do their work FOR them. Commission them and then watch as they rock not only your world but also the world around them.

Disney makes for great vacations; planning retreats make enable your family to identify and act on a shared vision.

Forget resolutions, they do not work. No successful organization runs on resolutions. Market share would drop, and eventually they'd go bankrupt.

Schedule your first retreat and go on it prepared to write because earth-shaking ideas that exist ONLY in your head haven't the magic needed to propel you forward. Write your ideas and plans down. Teach your family how to accomplish them. Actualize your plans.

You only live once. There's nothing worse than completing your planning exercises only to have your plan collect dust. Create a living vision. When someone asks you a career or life question or if you face a major decision, knowing your purpose will give you your answers.

What do you stand for? What's your vision?

CIO: Wake up and Lead

Alexander the Great, one of the greatest military generals who ever lived, conquered almost the entire known world with his vast army. As the story goes, one night during a campaign, he couldn't sleep and left his tent to walk the campgrounds. He came across a soldier asleep on guard duty—a serious offense.

The penalty for sleeping on guard duty was death. The soldier awoke as Alexander the Great approached. Recognizing who stood before him, the young man feared for his life.

Alexander the Great looked down at the soldier. "Do you know what the penalty is for sleeping on guard duty?"

"Yes, sir." The young man's voice quivered.

His features hardened, and Alexander the Great put a hand on the hilt of his sword. "What's your name, soldier?"

"Alexander, sir."

Alexander the Great studied the young man with a searing gaze. "What is your name?"

"My name is Alexander, sir." The soldier's knees shook.

A third time, Alexander the Great demanded, "What is your name?"

Breathing heavily, the young man replied, "My name is Alexander, sir."

Alexander the Great then looked the sentry in the face with great intensity. "Soldier, either change your name or change your conduct."

True or not, this story brings out the point that it's our duty to walk with the authority of our calling. As CIOs, we continually lobby for a voice at the table. We want to be seen and treated as a peer by our C-Suite counterparts. After interviewing several CEOs and CIOs, I found that in our quest to be recognized by the first letters of our title—typically VP (Vice President) or SVP (Senior Vice President)—we ultimately back down when the opportunity to be heard presents itself.

Notable exceptions exist. We all know CIOs who have gone on to lead other areas of their organizations such as human resources, strategy, finance (yes, *finance*), or construction, or have become CEOs. But these examples are rare.

Being a successful CIO means having a specific vision and sticking with it, not broadening it until it encompasses every aspect of the company's business

Here is a quick pulse check to figure out whether you are truly a leader among CIOs:

- Are you presently leading anything outside of IT?

- When you speak do you do so as a business person or a techie?

- Do you routinely showcase the business value of IT investments?

- Are you known to resolve challenges or do you run for cover?

- Do you frequently say, "There is no such thing as an IT project" and then punt your responsibility?

- Do you tell people you "lead from behind"?

Let's take an example many can relate to. Most CIOs in the healthcare industry are already on or are preparing to embark upon an EHR (Electronic Health Records) journey. What an opportunity to lead! Certainly, you do not have to lead alone, but you should never abdicate your leadership on this issue. Never forget that while the majority of troubled EHR initiatives were not led by CIOs, when things went wrong the CIO was usually the one who was let go. You may as well take the lead in areas that involve IT whenever possible because one way or another and despite any attempt to disassociate, the CIO is integral to almost every action taken by the business. You will take the fall! I advocate that you lead alongside others, not in front or behind!

So, you are all set to lead. Here are some critical success factors to consider:

- **Passion**. It is contagious. No passion = no energy. Nobody wants to follow a listless leader.

- **Visibility**. Be seen and heard. We rotate our leadership meetings within all our business units. At each meeting the host unit's business and clinical leaders are our special guests, and it excites them to see us on their turf.

- **Trust.** You know the old adage: do what you say you will do. It's tough to build trust. Straying from the truth breaks the bonds of trust.

- **Boldness.** Being a CIO is not for the faint of heart. Based on advice from my new team, I stopped an EHR implementation and insisted we regroup before the project went south. This timely timeout reestablished our path to a very successful implementation and enabled the kind of returns we had originally hoped for.

Let me close by asking you: What is your name? Or better yet, *what is your title?* If you are not leading, then downgrade your title. Either start acting like a leader or give someone else the opportunity! Healthcare is desperate for strong leaders, especially CIOs.

Brand Or Be Branded!

It was 1997. Reverberating rave music generated a hip vibe. Cameras flashed as the crowd studied the student models. I was attending my first fashion show, and sat at the end of the runway—as one of the judges. The dean of my alma mater had appointed me to the board of the fashion school (long story). I and my fellow judges—all of whom were in the fashion business—were responsible for appraising the graduate-students' designs. Despite my initial excitement at the opportunity to be a fashion critic, I quickly realized my business skills didn't match well with my responsibility. If you had ever seen my tie collection, you would understand. I felt as out of place as a punk rocker at symphony hall.

But I did gain one valuable lesson from that experience. The beauty of a model or her/his clothing design didn't captivate me. The confidence with which the model walked did. The runway models defined the brand more than did the fabrics or colors.

Whether or not you embrace it, the cold hard truth is that you are judged, and you are judged daily. Unless you establish your brand, your board, executive team, peers, subordinates and business associates will do the branding for you. In fact, you already have a brand and may not even know it. That work's been done for you by others. Rather than accept a label given to you behind your back, take responsibility and define and project your own brand.

My friends in marketing say: *brand* or be *branded*. Begin with some intensive soul searching, then decide on the brand you wish to project. Examine your life. Ensure that your chosen brand is aligned with your core competencies and your personal vision.

Once you've defined your brand, here are a few ideas for enhancing and managing it:

- **Network.** Continually expand your professional and personal networks. Proactively reaching out to others prevents isolation and decreases the risk of irrelevancy. There are many avenues for building your networks, including LinkedIn, Twitter and Facebook.

- **Publish.** Editors are interested in genuine stories from real leaders. Send queries and don't give up if rejected.

- **Present.** Get over your fears. Presenting forces you to succinctly nail down your subject matter, and makes you confront your doubts. Seize opportunities to appear before professional societies, neighborhood associations, your place of worship and before your subordinates, peers and superiors at your place of work

- **Involvement.** Jump into the community. Let the other leaders know you're interested in adding value.

- **Volunteer.** Seek out regular opportunities, and you will find more people to network with.

- **Routinely Self-Review.** Schedule time to review progress and make adjustments. Ask for feedback and use it to update your brand while finetuning your career strategic plan. If you don't have a plan, find a mentor.

- **Education.** Take the initiative to self-educate. Learn from inside and outside of IT and healthcare.

- **Add to Your Existing Body of Knowledge.** Interact with others and learn from that interaction.

No action will spoil your brand faster than damaged credibility. So while I'm all about a personal hallmark, it must be built upon a solid foundation of execution and excellence. These are not sequential tasks. Proactively improve performance and brand simultaneously.

Critics will say your brand is created and reinforced by your actions. This holds some truth, but it would be foolhardy not to be deliberate. Please! Take a look at politics for a moment as we head into another presidential election cycle. According to a study in *The Journal of Personality and Social Psychology*, when evaluating others, people prefer the *potential* of an individual over their past accomplishments. I maintain that this propensity for potential is stimulated by an effective brand.

Keep your brand in perspective, and let it humble you. The value of a stellar brand should reach far beyond you, and its primary benefits should accrue to the people and the organization served. If not, then it's only about you. Possessing a personal brand is key to success. It should never come from arrogance or false humility. If you do not establish your brand, you are allowing others to determine both your brand and, potentially, your future.

You're on the runway, lights flashing, cameras clicking. You may not always be able to select the clothes, but you must maintain poise and grace. Make no mistake; the crowd is analyzing your every step. So brand yourself and accentuate your brand with confidence.

CIO UNPLUGGED...UNPLUGGED

"Aim high, aim for something that will make a difference, rather than for something that is safe and easy to do."

– Peter Drucker

How are you wired? Have you studied yourself lately or are you too busy tearing down others so as to build up your worth?

Experiences give shape to character, bringing out what's already inside—the genuine you. How you and I react to life's events—both good or bad—determine whether we will find success or failure. You were created to succeed, but have you *chosen* to be less? James Kouzes, a leading authority on leadership, has said "Leaders are honest, forward-looking, competent, and inspiring."

Be Honest. As a college freshman, I definitely hit rock bottom. I had a GPA of 1.6 and a bank account drained by my party life. Friends? Maybe. Family? Far away. College was an empty, hauntingly painful experience. I could see where I was headed and I wanted none of it. With nothing left to lose, I made the decision to embark on the greatest adventure of all—a new life, free at last. In my junior year, the adventure accelerated and I married. Not just any woman. Julie was and is valiant, vulnerable and scandalous. She keeps my feet on the ground. We said "no" to the safe life, and our journey has continued for 29 years and counting.

Say "No" to simply existing. The easy life makes zero difference to the rest of humanity. Healthcare IT has enough technology or talk about bits and bytes. What healthcare IT needs is bold leadership!

Be Inspiring. A great adventure is thrilling and dangerous. Whether climbing mountains, swimming in oceans, preparing for war or competing at the highest levels, I've done it, and I worked my butt off to accomplish each of my goals. I've taken roles that stretched me and then asked for more, still trembling from my last achievement. Standing up to bullies takes guts, but someone has to do it. I will, and I have. I've expanded employers' guardrails—how else could they have room to grow?

Three times I've faced death. Reprimands await me around every corner. I've questioned myself and my motives. I may fail, but I will bounce back. I make myself a target. So why do I keep going? Because I understand who I am, what my purpose is, and why I was created. I have a vision for my life. I accept the downside knowing the upside will be rewarding. The safe life is not worth living.

My mission is to "Leverage information technology and leadership to improve people's health." My vision is to "Develop Information Technology leaders who impact organizations." My writing about leadership from a CIO's perspective is one of my strategies to make my mission and vision into realities. The feedback I have received helps measure my progress. People have sent me stories that made me cry, others had me shouting for joy. Their stories tell about how they took a stand, or rose to their potential. I have received stories from vendor and hospital CEOs, from clinicians, from the young and the old. Modeling and encouraging leadership influences more people than any comments I have made about technology. Even in Information Technology leadership is about the leading, and not the wiring.

The significant way to transform healthcare is to speak less on technology and instead be a leader with a bias for action. You can learn about the cloud, networks, or virtualization in school. Leadership, on the other hand, is caught not taught. I will not waste energy rehashing Computers 301 when I can challenge and inspire you to be more of who you were created to be: A success!

Do you have a defined purpose? Are you actively pursuing *your* vision for *your* life and career? How do you measure your results? What motivates you?

TAKING CONTROL OF YOUR DESTINY

For me, the capstone of holiday seasons past has been "the Plunge"—leaping into the icy waters of Lake Erie wearing nothing but swim trunks. Each New Year's Day, we triathlon club members gingerly—if not insanely—work our way across the snow and ice then charge into the lake. Once we reach waist-high water, we crown our feat with a head first dive. Like an arctic baptism, "the Plunge" magically washes away the old and welcomes the new.

Another holiday tradition my family has practiced for many years is strategic planning retreats. Each of us, from the oldest to the youngest, evaluate and polish our personal plans. I first learned about the power of planning while studying business in graduate school. Later, in my first few jobs, I observed how leadership teams carved out time each year to develop and hone mission and vision statements, which always included values and objectives. These teams jetted off to exotic locations offering sunshine and sand or posh mountain lodges. Liberated from work distractions, they would rate their company's performance against these plans and make adjustments for the following year.

Literature searches provided ample evidence that businesses with a solid planning process significantly outperformed their non-planning peers. I soon asked myself, "Could these planning principles be applied to my life? My marriage. My family?"

The Marx family's strategic planning adventure started modestly. Short, inexpensive, trips away from home reduced distraction and stimulated creativity. These trips eventually morphed into more elaborate excursions, but the focus always remained on strategic planning.

Since beginning this process, we have experienced dramatic increases in the quality of our careers, relationships and life. Even as preteens, our children possessed a solid knowledge of who they were, where they were going and what they needed to accomplish in order to fulfill their calling. We signed our plans and lived by them.

I'm astonished at the number of organizations, divisions and individuals not guided by a written plan. What is the standard by which they measure success? What foundations and principles are ensuring their sound investments and decision-making? What is the vision that brings out their passion and gives them a sense of purpose? Do they know the end game? Which values serve as beacons to ensure integrity?

Earth-shaking ideas that exist only in a leader's head are not enough. He or she must write them down. Teach them. Actualize them. Moreover, there is nothing worse than going through planning exercises merely to have the plan collect dust. He or she must create a living vision!

Plunging into annual end-of-year processes and preparations for the upcoming year, my encouragement to you is to spend some thoughtful time reviewing planning. If you don't have a strategic information systems plan, or one that is embedded in the overall business plan, then get out your calendar today. Block out time to work with your staff and key stakeholders to initiate this critical process. You cannot effectively lead your organization without one. The old must go so the new can thrive.

On the personal side, pack up your family, get out of town, and spend time in a setting where beauty can inspire you. Arctic baptism not required! Just find a place free from distractions. Sit down with your family and design a mission and vision together. Let the kids submit values by which all can live. Help them develop lifelong strategies and objectives, as opposed to New Year's resolutions that have the shelf life of unrefrigerated eggs.

Give yourself and the ones you love a most amazing New Year's gift: a vision, a plan, and the means for you and them to take control of your destiny!

3
BELIEVE IN SOMETHING BIGGER THAN YOU: GRACE, GUIDANCE, FAITH

faith (fāth), n.
1. confidence or trust in a person or thing: *faith in another's ability.* 2. belief that is not based on proof: *He had faith that the hypothesis would be substantiated by fact.* 3. belief in God or in the doctrines or teachings of religion: *the firm faith of the Pilgrims.*

We all can use help.

When I ponder all the challenges in my life I can't imagine relying on just my own strength and wisdom. While I leverage numerous resources and friends throughout life, even that has limits.

It has been my personal experience that my faith in God has provided the foundation and fuel for all of my success and extraordinary tales. God is the one constant who never changes.

The role of faith in my life is very important. My faith has given me guidance, grace and a foundation for my life. I have screwed up many times in my life but my faith has always helped me to recover from those bad decisions and let me make them right.

I was raised as a Catholic, but I really found my faith when I went off to college. During my freshman year, my roommates and I got into a discussion about faith. I had been thinking more and more about my relationship with God. We talked for a long time about what faith meant to us and eventually we began praying together. That was the start for me; faith became a major part of my life from that point forward.

I met my wife Julie at about the same time. She was going through a similar phase in her life. We found a church and got involved in campus ministry. It drew us together and continues to do so. From then on things in my life began to change.

My faith is very important to me. I don't hide it, but neither do I impose it on others. It is a part of my personal vision statement: "I want to live my life in such a manner as to directionally point people towards faith."

I try to live my faith in all aspects of my life.

LEADERSHIP AND RECONCILIATION

I get knocked on my ass every now and again. Okay… it happens often.

My big fall took place a few years ago. Grace and mercy picked me up, as they always do. God changed my life direction, and I still haven't gotten over it. God's grace and mercy made me a thankful person; He taught me to be a builder of others. I strive to be humble, and consistently fall short (just ask my wife). I'm very much a work in progress. I stay on the path, I keep my chin up. When I think too long about my journey, I get weepy. Success has come more by grace and mercy than from skill or talent; in many respects my success has been unearned.

These realizations set the stage for me to pursue reconciliation as a leadership practice.

I started this process with my family years ago. I knew I had hurt those dearest to me, so I went to them to reconcile. Today, there is nothing left hidden or unsaid, at least on my end. Then I remembered all the people I had treated poorly in high school, college and throughout my career. I sought them out, told them I was sorry and asked what I could do to make things right. Most were receptive. Many relationships were restored. Not all. I did what I could and moved on.

In workplaces where I had sown hatred, envy, bitterness, malice, brokenness—I reversed course and made amends. In some cases, I did so by extending grace and mercy as I it had been given to me. In most cases, I asked for forgiveness and sought ways to reverse the damages inflicted. Not long ago, I failed in that respect big time, and it haunts me still. I'm compelled to share this with you so you can learn from my mistake.

My 2005 mentor, Dr. Achilles Demetriou, died recently. I am who I am in part because of his profound influence on my development as an executive. We had an incredible relationship that was disrupted by my departure from University Hospitals in 2007. We were at a critical juncture in our deployment of an EHR (Electronic Health Records) initiative, and I knew my decision to leave upset him in particular. Achilles and I were partnered to ensure success. My timing was imperfect; we both knew it. While I received support and encouragement from others when I moved on, Achilles was physically and emotionally absent. I needed to reconcile but I never did and now it's too late. This saddened me on many levels. Foremost, we had all lost a great man, leader, scientist, and clinician. But the pain cut deeper for me. I lost the opportunity to talk through stuff, make peace, and renew a relationship that shaped me.

May it never happen again!

What about you? As you read this, do any names come to mind? Family? Friends? Co-workers? Who do you need to reconcile with?

Making peace with people doesn't just *happen*. It takes a pro-active effort. Reconciliation comes down to leadership. If you're a leader, *you make the first move*. Don't wait for the other person because there is no guarantee that will happen. Break out of your emotional prison and reach out to the other person.

I challenge you, my colleagues. As names come to mind, write them down. In the next 24 hours, reach out to each person on your list. Not every attempt will turn out rosy, but you will have done the right thing. In many cases, you will achieve a restoration of something lost from your life. Your call, card, or visit might trigger a transformation or breakthrough in someone else's life. It will definitely be transformative in yours. This is leadership at its best, and at its hardest. Be humble.

Reconcile *before death robs you of that opportunity*, and you'll escape the pain that haunts me. Believe in something bigger than yourself and recompense your way to freedom.

A SACRED CALLING

"The Human contribution is the essential ingredient. It is only in giving of one's self to others that we truly live."

— *Ethel Percy Andrus*

Someone asked our Chief Medical Information Officer, Ferdinand Velasco, M.D., why he would leave his skyrocketing career as a cardiac surgeon at New York-Presbyterian to become CMIO with our organization. I will never forget his answer. "As a heart surgeon, I could help about 200 people per year. As CMIO, I am helping the 6.2 million people in our region."

Whether we give direct care or support someone who does, we are fulfilling a sacred calling by touching human lives. Don't discount information technology because it's *only computer stuff and nobody really knows where cyberspace is anyway*. You could have practiced IT in any industry, yet you chose healthcare. Or, perhaps, healthcare chose you.

Sacred callings come in various forms. Although healthcare IT is nothing unique in and of itself, there is an element of sanctity that draws and keeps me in our field. If we want to live a life of significance, we must understand there is a passion to our calling and remember that our work matters. Grasp that it is a privilege to serve humanity with your skills and talents. To serve is sacred.

In using our hands for work—answering service desk calls, pulling cables, creating order sets, managing projects, developing strategies, creating apps—we are helping those who care for the patients and clinicians. We're telling them, "Your work is important to us and we value what you do."

Stop for a moment. Reread the above paragraph then hold your hands in front of you. While studying your hands, reflect on what they do each day that contributes to caring for the health needs in your community. Seriously. Have you not chosen to *bless* others through the work of your hands?

Wherever people are involved (life), challenges and frustrations exist. Healthcare is beset with issues. We remain focused during those difficult circumstances by remembering our purpose and our vision. Let me share with you one recent technique we developed to maintain the heart-to-head connection.

Blessing of the Hands. It is not unusual for hospitals to conduct non-denominational *Blessing of the Hands* ceremonies. I have seen this done for clinicians at one of our hospitals, and it got me to thinking, *what about IT?* Our work is no less critical to the healing process. IT hands may not touch patients, but we do touch their lives in unseen ways. Arguably, IT is the only segment of healthcare that touches the *entire* healthcare continuum.

I contacted our chaplains and they were excited by the concept. This spring for the first time we conducted a *Blessing of the Hands* ceremony exclusively for

IT. The chaplains first shared with our team the sanctity of what we do in serving people and the impact we have on the lives of both patients and caregivers. They prayed over us. They prayed a blessing over a special vial of oil and then used it to anoint our hands. One at a time, we rose from our seats and approached the chaplains. While we held open our hands, they anointed them and gave us each a verbal blessing. I sat back down and allowed this special moment to fully soak in. I imagine many others felt as renewed as I did.

All I can say is that it was a holy moment for all who chose to participate, regardless of their religious orientation or belief system. We emerged inspired and empowered. We walked out of there *knowing* that we were making a difference in the lives of others every day.

Below is a sample *Blessing of the Hands* prayer. This *Blessing of the Hands* is from *In Praise of Hands*, by Diann Neu, from *Waterwheel*, Winter 1989, adapted by Corlette Pierson, Pastoral Care Resident at Rush-Presbyterian-St. Luke's Medical Center, Chicago.

Blessed be these hands that have touched life.
Blessed be these hands that have felt pain.
Blessed be these hands that have embraced with compassion.
Blessed be these hands that have been clinched with anger or withdrawn in fear.
Blessed be these hands that have drawn blood and administered medicine.
Blessed be these hands that have cleaned beds and disposed of wastes.
Blessed be these hands that have anointed the sick and offered blessings.
Blessed be these hands that grow stiff with age.
Blessed be these hands that have comforted the dying and held the dead.
Blessed be these hands that develop applications that improve quality of care.
Blessed be these hands that answer the phone and empathize while solving issues.
Blessed be these hands that reprogram the broken network.

Blessed be these hands that enable life-saving technology.
Blessed be these hands, we hold the future in these hands.
Blessed be our hands for they are the work of Your hands, O Holy One.

No matter what your area (supplier, payor or provider), I highly encourage you as a leader to make this voluntary ceremony available for your teams. You'll witness a demonstrable impact, and you'll be reminded that what *you* do is significant. Your calling is sacred.

GO TO GROW

In 2008, I dropped off my oldest child at Biola University in Southern California. We arrived a few days early so my son Brandon and I could attend student/parent orientations together.

During our free time—and in the name of father/son tradition—we squeezed in some workouts and ate bad but tasty food. After we got his belongings organized in his dorm, we huddled for a final prayer and blessing, embraced and shed a man tear or two, and then I left. Sitting in my car in the parking lot, I watched him walk to the final student orientation. At home while he was growing up I had planted seeds; I encouraged him to grow, to test his personal boundaries, and I discouraged signs of complacency. Brandon had officially begun his journey into the future and to independence, and the results of my optimistic seed planting were soon to blossom.

What happened next surprised me. As I drove down the Pacific Coast Highway, I began to wail. From the depths of my soul, I cried so hard my stomach convulsed. Wheezing in breaths, I mourned my treasured son's rite of passage. Then my mourning turned to dancing, and I rejoiced for Brandon and his future. I can only imagine what the drivers in the cars next to me must have been thinking of this spectacle.

As time passed, we have seen amazing growth in our son, growth that could not have occurred had he stayed home. Despite an enriching and loving environment, his potential would not be fully realized without dramatic change and new challenges. We would have loved to have him stay, but we knew, and accepted that he needed to go to grow.

My career has been much the same. I can't think of a single employer that I have ever *wanted* to leave. Yet with each employer, I knew at some point I'd need to *go to grow*. Indisputably, my former employers offered ample career growth and challenges, but for exponential and accelerated growth, I had to embark on a journey—break out of my comfort zones and push the envelope of security.

Each successive move has pushed me out of my natural inclination toward complacency. These moves have shaped and sharpened my abilities. The breadth and depth of new and divergent experiences have broadened my skill set in extraordinary ways. My talents have gained a sharper focus, and my leadership quotient has multiplied. I attribute my growth, both personally and professionally, to my pushing of boundaries and circumvention of the traditional career path.

I believe it is a leader's imperative to fight complacency in the workplace and to encourage others to *go to grow*. If going to grow benefits our children and ourselves, then we must be willing to encourage subordinates and peers to do the same. Does this sound inconceivable? Untraditional? Scary? Of course we need to create internal opportunities and provide career ladders, to offer options to every kind of employee. Yet, at some point, the best thing for some will be a new environment, a place that challenges them to accelerate to the next level. An exceptional leader is not afraid or insecure to let their best go so that they too may grow.

I have helped some of my best employees go to grow. I have referred opportunities to them for external advancement and then served as their reference. With each departure, I felt a collegial loss of their skills and talents, and sometimes even cried in secret; yet I never regretted a single endorsement. I've stayed in touch, and have known the thrill of seeing them grow in ways far more enriching than could have been realized from any opportunities I or my employer could have offered. They had to *go to grow* to reach their fullest potential.

Are there people in your life and work who need to *go to grow?* Does complacency have a hold on your organization? Are you selfishly clinging, or do you have the heart to make available opportunities to your best and brightest? (Picture an able-bodied forty-year-old son or daughter still living at home.) If one of your staff has significant potential but circumstances are such that you cannot fully exploit that potential, do you give them the freedom to look for advancement elsewhere? Are there other staff members who need your encouragement to leave for these same reasons but who won't do so out of fear? Help them realize their vision and at the same time you will realize your own.

We have a few years left with our teenage daughter and we will cherish every minute. But we'll also do our best to prepare her to take on the challenges and opportunities that enrich our lives. In love, we will push her to learn from the past and will let her fail forward, maximizing her present to prepare her for the future. Ultimately, the time will come when she will *go to grow,* just like her brother.

Now it's your turn. *Go to grow!*

4

BUILD A TEAM OF LIFE GIVERS: MENTOR AND MARRY WELL

men • tor (men'tôr), n.
1. a wise and trusted counselor or teacher. 2. an influential senior sponsor or supporter.

They say the world is divided into two kinds of people: life givers and life takers. Life givers love you and support you. Life takers are, well, just that—those who are only in a relationship for themselves and will take everything they can from it. Life takers can bleed you of your time, energy and resources.

Never forget, you tend to become like those you spend the most time with. Too much time with life takers may change your own motivations. I am very careful about which people I hang out with. It is said that you become most like the four people you hang out with most.

Hang out with life givers. Build a team of them. Life is hard, marriage is really hard. You need life givers to help you get through it all. As a couple, my wife and I work very hard to hang out with other couples who feel the same way as we do, couples who, like us, are life givers.

I am into mentoring—both mentoring others and being mentored. I've benefited from mentors all my professional life. Mine are formal mentors—we

Wife Julie jumped up on our kitchen counter to surprise me in her new catwoman costume she had purchased for an upcoming party. Colleyville, TX Oct 2013

draw up an agreement and for a specific period of time. These contracts are structured and usually for one year, which means I now have fifteen mentors I can go back and consult with. I mentor others as well. I believe in this kind of relationship very strongly.

I am fortunate that I married well, and that my wife is my biggest fan and supporter. She is so amazing, a wonderful person and life giver. We got married very young (when were both twenty) and while I did not then fully appreciate how lucky I was, I do now. We based our relationship and our decision to get married on our faith. It was very important to us both and we both wanted to pursue our faith together.

I can not imagine, had I not married well, how much more difficult and challenging life would have been.

THE LOST ART OF MENTORING

Who taught you your life skills? Did anyone coach you in the ways of culture and values? Was it an uncle? Your grandma? The television?

I just watched the movie *Gran Torino* with Clint Eastwood. In a nutshell, Eastwood attempts to teach an immigrant neighbor boy how to be a man. He starts by teaching the boy, Thao, the skill of carpentry, how to hold a hammer and which tools to always have on hand. Then he comically endeavors to educate the kid on manly talk and how to act like a man. Eastwood verbalizes it, then demonstrates it, and finally observes Thao doing what he'd learned. This mission takes time, money, and energy, but they forge a relationship that proves worthy of their efforts.

Some of us wish we had had that kind of mentoring experience. Speaking from experience, I believe we all *need* mentors. When I became CIO of a large, prestigious organization while still in my mid-thirties, I was both elated and scared. What helped me to become comfortable and successful as a CIO was the mentorship I received. Even now with much more experience, I find that a mentor is essential to my continued growth.

Dictionary.com defines mentoring as "…an ongoing, planned partnership that focuses on helping a person reach specific goals over a period of time." Unfortunately, the art of mentoring has not caught on in the business world, healthcare included. We see this reflected specifically in the graying of existing leadership and the lack of succession planning.

This type of one-on-one interaction between individuals—lost somewhere after the apprenticeships of the pre-industrial age—has been replaced with short-term, focused leadership programs. These programs attempt to turbo-charge management education by cramming years of collective wisdom into a one-week program. For example, the College of Healthcare Information Management Executives (CHIME) has an excellent leadership development program entitled "The CIO Boot Camp." CHIME cannot keep up with the demand for enrollment. One reason for its popularity? It fills the mentoring void that exists in many organizations.

Is Mentoring Beneficial in Healthcare? Done right, both formal and informal mentoring programs promote patient safety and facilitate clinical process change. Mentoring is a key aspect of building alliances within an organization, ensuring the development of a new generation of trained leaders. Committing to mentor another person is an investment in the long-term success of your organization; it is a selfless act of service for the sake of our profession and the future of healthcare.

This type of partnering also offers something a person might not get directly from their supervisor: broader experience, organizational perspective, and new skills.

For instance, an Information Technology professional will benefit greatly from having a CFO or CNO (Chief Nursing Officer) as a mentor. Consider the differences between learning the technical aspects of your position and career versus learning leadership from someone else in authority, regardless of his background. In other words, an IT person should not enter a mentoring relationship with another IT person, lest the broader lessons risk being drowned in the technical minutiae IT is so famous for.

Selecting an Appropriate Mentor. Examine your strengths and weaknesses. A professional who lacks a strong clinical background should seek out a CMO/CNO or another well-respected clinician. Conversely, someone who already has a strong clinical background may want to seek out a CFO in order to gain key insights into the financial side of healthcare. Seeking such mentors within your own organization offers the advantage of proximity and familiarity. Furthermore, the development of such relationships assists in the overall development of teamwork and connectedness. Mentors from outside of the organization or healthcare field might offer a level of anonymity and broad perspective, but they would also lack meaningful context for key elements of discussions.

Mentoring Programs and Recruiting. Job candidates respond favorably when they understand that the organization cares about their professional development and wishes to enable career success. Over time, as the mentoring program becomes a major differentiator in recruitment efforts, your organization will become an employer of choice. The Gallup organization has statistically demonstrated that an organization with a high level of engaged employees significantly outperforms non-engaged workforces in areas encompassing customer satisfaction and financial results—resulting in a win for both employee and employer. Clearly, such programs lead to improved corporate health.

Mentoring Enables Clinical, Business, and IT Success. Most IT leaders have a clear understanding of their task: to leverage technology to enable clinical and financial success.

Much of this understanding however resides in knowledge and not transformative experience. Clinical mentoring, for example, facilitates the adoption and understanding of what really takes place in a clinical setting. The IT leader gets first-hand experience and sees with their own eyes what they had only heard or read about.

Partnering an IT leader with a CMO or CNO exposes them to new insights and understanding. One academic medical center I know sends its IT leaders on

48

annual short-term mentoring assignments to all of its clinical departments including ED, Radiology, Lab, etc. The CIO experiences routine rounds with physicians and residents. The mentor allows the IT leader to experience the specific clinical care setting, answers questions, and discusses the critical intersection of IT and quality patient care. As a result, IT leaders come back with a new sense of purpose and motivation. In turn they make immediate changes to IT systems and support to help ensure a higher quality of care.

Mentoring serves to develop future IT leaders. Given the limited pool of emerging leaders, mentoring has become more critical than ever. Identifying and growing talent within our organizations is imperative. Our leadership effectiveness is not so much based on formal education and rigorous reading, but in on-the-job experiences. Partnering up-and-coming IT leaders with other members of your executive leadership team facilitates this real life experience, accelerates growth, and ensures the success of critical succession planning.

Restoring Lost Arts. We are the sum of our collective inputs. I credit my success to my mentors. I have been deliberate in this process. In even years, I mentor someone; in odd years, I am mentored. I require each of my direct reports to do likewise. I've been formally mentored by health system CEOs, COOs, CFOs, CMOs and hospital Presidents. I have mentored many who have since moved into positions of greater authority. Research for yourself the many resources available on establishing quality mentoring programs.

MENTORING 2.0

When I accepted the 2013 HIMSS/CHIME John E. Gall Jr. Award as CIO of the Year, three of my mentors were sitting at my table. I asked them to be with me because these men had coached me during key phases of my personal and professional life. Mentoring is everything to me. Everything.

I have given a dozen speeches around the country on mentoring. I am passionate on the topic because it shaped who I am today and where I will be tomorrow. I want to share with you one method to accelerate the adoption of mentoring in your organization, to help you get to "Mentoring 2.0."

My colleagues and I created the Business Technology Leadership Academy (BTLA) several years ago. Its purpose is to accelerate and enhance the pipeline that produces business technology leaders at all levels in our organization. The curriculum is designed to prepare candidates to take on positions of increasing responsibility by developing and sharpening their leadership skills. Major props to our People & Culture (HR) division who helped make the BTLA vision a reality.

Format. The Academy lasts ten months during which my direct reports and I serve as mentors.

Seminars. The Academy meets once a month for two hours. The first meeting focuses on developing relationships and establishing the rules of the road. Student (Mentee) goals are agreed upon based on 360-degree feedback, developmental needs, and career objectives. Both mentor and mentee sign a contract. This covenant identifies the specific roles and responsibilities of both parties with outcomes clearly identified. The next eight seminars focus on the eight BTLA "Success Factors."

Individual Sessions. Each month the mentor and mentee meet privately for ninety minutes. There are few rules that apply but the time is focused to help the mentee discuss real world situations they have faced and how they impact defined goals. Time is also spent on development of assigned presentations and special projects.

Shadow Opportunities. Mentees have the opportunity to spend more time with their mentors through shadowing. This provides more time for coaching while giving the mentee a chance to see their mentor in action. Often, the best mentoring occurs when nothing is said, but much is observed. Mentees participate in our leadership meetings, off-site retreats, attend conferences and observe their mentor's presentations.

Professional Development. Students are automatically enrolled in any special development activities we might have during their course, including high impact presentation classes and personal development courses.

Special Projects. Students are expected to volunteer for special projects. These will vary and must be agreed upon by both mentor and mentee. A student might help lead our annual TEDx event while another leads our organization's annual employee giving campaign. These projects provide real-world opportunities for leadership while under the careful eye of a mentor and are ideal for real-time coaching.

Selection. Selection is a highly competitive process. Every employee is encouraged to apply. We have an average of 100 applications each year. We have an online questionnaire consisting of roughly twenty questions. There are no right or wrong answers, but some answers receive a higher point value than others, but prospective students are not aware of which questions nor do they know that some questions are weighted. Typically, the twenty-five submissions that score highest are selected for the next round which peer and manager review focused. Once those results are in, we look at the final twelve or so candidates. Our People & Culture team runs special reports for us that provide additional insight into each prospective student. With all the data points in hand, my team then vigorously debates which candidates to select for that year's cohort. We try to ensure a diversity of individuals with respect to title, responsibilities, and gender. After the finalists are decided upon, we debate further to determine the mentor/mentee combinations. Again, we use leadership's judgment to make the best matches possible. We have few rules, but one is that the mentor may not already be in the mentee's chain of command. The benefit of this rule is significant cross-pollination. For instance, we may have an applications vice president mentor a technical analyst or our CTO may have a governance manager as a mentee.

Criteria. Applicants always want to know the specific criteria and scoring formulas we utilize. We purposefully do not share these. We do not want candidates gaming their applications to maximize point values.

Expectations. Clearly, we are making a material investment in our students. Joining BTLA requires the applicant to make a long-term commitment to our organization. It also means that, when calls for volunteers are made, BTLA graduates should be the first to respond. There is nothing worse than investing but getting no return. Mentors are expected to make their mentee a top priority and are making a significant time and mind investment. And while we want our BTLA graduates to stay with us for a long time, we do ultimately realize that sometimes people need to move on from our organization to achieve their true potential. We believe in "go to grow."

Outcomes. We have observed tremendous growth in our inaugural cohort. They are more confident and effective. By continuing this program we will multiply the leadership capabilities of our IT organization ten-fold. But there is another reason we do BTLA. We, the mentors, learn. We may in fact learn more than the students!

My hope is that, one day, a few years from now, one of our graduates will be accepting an important award, and their mentor will be sitting at the table cheering them on! Just as mine did that evening not so long ago.

***The Business Technology Leadership Academy (BTLA) is the property of Texas Health Resources, all rights reserved.*

THE CONNECTERS...

For six-year-old Herbert, a train ride was nothing new. But this train was different. Cold. Smelly. No seats. The conductors wore helmets, carried guns and yelled. Shrouded in darkness and smushed between people's legs, Herbert clung to his mother and aunt. Passengers wept and prayed. Days later, they disembarked at the internment camp known as Gurs in southwestern France.

Horrid scarcely described the inhumane conditions in the "relocation" camp. Herbert dug through the trash each day, foraging for crumbs. Six months into the torment, a German solider grabbed him and carried him outside the camp gates. The French Resistance, hiding in the night, whisked Herb into the woods. Dodging armed patrols, they traversed the countryside and came to a convent near Lyon—Herbert's new home. During routine inspections, the nuns hid him, the only Jew amongst Gentiles. A year later, the Swiss underground led him on foot over the Alps into Switzerland where he found solace in a group home for Jewish boys. Herb never saw his family again. While he scaled mountains to freedom, they boarded trains for Auschwitz.

After the war, Red Cross officials connected Herbert with relatives that had immigrated to the United States years prior. A young adolescent, fluent in French and German, Herb sailed across the Atlantic. Lady Liberty greeted him in the New York harbor. He learned English, and five years later, Herbert returned to Germany as an American soldier. He fell in love with a young fräulein. They had seven children. I am the youngest.

At the end of each year, I reflect and give thanks for many things in my personal and professional life. I'm grateful for what I call *The Connecters:* the beautiful people who held my dad's hand. From the German guard at Gurs who led him through freedom's gate, to the hands of the men and women of the underground. For the nuns who loved a boy of a different faith. For the schoolmasters who hid my father in defiance of the law and for the hands of my immigrant uncle who welcomed him into his New Jersey home. They connected my father to his future. In my heart, I kiss those hands.

This year, my gratitude focuses on my own personal Connecters, those who helped and enabled my then-future career. While hiring me didn't affect life or death, I am thankful to those who took a gamble on me. Here are my Connecters and what they taught me:

Pastor Rick Olmstead. In a small but growing church, Pastor Rick invited everyone from the congregation who had an interest in leadership to his home for a BBQ. He'd hoped for gray heads but instead got four young-in-their-faith college sophomores. Trusting in a higher power, Rick pushed forward and invested in us. We eventually became part of the team that enabled our church to experience multi-year, double-digit growth. His exceptional mentoring and leadership formed the foundation of who I am today.

Major Loomis, Executive Officer, 244th Army Reserve Engineer Battalion. His additional duties included overseeing the Cadet program. As a nervous 19-year-old combat medic, I interviewed with him for one of the coveted Cadet slots. I knew others interviewed better than I did, but he took a chance and showed me unmerited favor. I went on to become a combat engineer officer. Upon earning the rank of captain, I served as the battalion motor officer and battalion movement officer. I learned much about organization, leadership, and process.

Mary Hein. She agreed to interview me because she had misread one of my degrees. She thought I had a Master's in Computer Science when in fact it was a Master's in Consumer Science. When I brought this to her attention, she let it pass and continued the interview. I had very little experience to speak of yet she offered me my first salaried professional position. I cried (not in front of her, of course). Mary taught me poise, communication and branding, and helped hone my leadership skills.

Mike Gogola. I was interviewing for a Director of Physician Relations position when I realized it was actually an IT position. "You have the wrong person," I told him. While I was good at physician relations and marketing, IT was not my forte. To this day, I'm not sure if he was desperate or sincere, but Mike assured me I had the right stuff for the position. He surrounded me with good technical people, and I learned on the go. Mike took me with him to networking opportunities and conferences. He taught me project management and IT.

Kevin Roberts. Kevin believed in me before anyone else saw my executive potential. He took a major risk in supporting my bid to become a CIO at a young age and without the requisite experience. He shielded me from naysayers as I learned to walk and then run. He pushed me to become increasingly independent, which grew my confidence. He believed in me.

I'm thankful for the men and women who saved my dad and made my life possible. And I'm thankful for the men and women who connected me, taking a risk, and enabling my career.

Who are you thankful for? Take the time to show them your appreciation.

But don't stop there. Ask yourself who you can help connect. When is the last time you took a risk to help an eager wannabe advance?

EVOLVING IT FROM TRANSACTIONAL TO TRANSFORMATIONAL

My most important mentor, the late Achilles Demetriou, had a profound impact on how I envision and operationalize healthcare IT. He did that by teaching me to think like a CEO.

"Ed," he would say, "to be an effective executive—a CIO—you need to think like Tom (our CEO). You need to understand his challenges, his pain points, and then make recommendations to help him handle these. When you do this, you will enable IT to make the leap from transactional to transformational." I credit his advice for helping me evolve my IT department in a way that has had an impact on many more lives than it otherwise would have.

Since he gave me this advice a decade ago, I have made it a priority to understand my CEO's vision and challenges. In addition to hearing from my CEO directly, I use other sources to give me a glimpse into the collective thoughts of my and other healthcare CEOs.

I frequently review the American College of Healthcare Executives' annual listing of top concerns. I challenge my peers to be more aware of their need to know their CEO's pain points. Sometimes I ask them to name the top concerns of their hospital's leadership. In my experience, few of my peers can list more than three, which tells me they simply aren't aware of their leadership's overall concerns.

To truly assist your CEO in meeting each challenge, IT must work hand in glove with the business side to suggest transformative solutions to overcome current and future obstacles.

IT can sit back all day long and pump out transactional solutions that may be helpful (more often they are not), but never help a department achieve its full potential. Solutions worth implementing present themselves only when IT and other administrative areas mutually engage one another and grow to understand one another.

I recall one time when our IT department thought we had hit a home run with our approach to training. Actually, our approach proved to be pretty good, but the result was more like hitting a single. Not until we engaged the business side (clinicians in particular) could we develop an innovative training approach that enabled our successfully implementation of EHRs (electronic health records initiatives) in both inpatient and outpatient settings. The organization-wide impact was transformational—a home run!

Hitting a home run happens when IT understands the challenges facing operations and then fully engage in a collaborative effort. Alignment becomes automatic. Transformation occurs. Everyone wins.

Thank you, Achilles.

REACH

I arrived at the bar early, a bit after five. I was already sipping Merlot as my first guest arrived. We'd never met before. In fact, I'd never met any of my guests. I'd found their contact information just a few weeks before and fired off an email invite. I had no idea who, if anyone, would show. We had little in common, so what could I expect from them?

Our connection? Their CEOs sat on the Board of my healthcare system.

Every first-year CIO is a rookie, but given my age I was a rookie among rookies. My first leadership endeavor was the selection and deployment of an electronic health record (EHR). What had I gotten myself into? I chosen to guide us through the biggest transformational challenge in the 140-year history of our organization. No pressure!

The guests I had invited to the bar all showed up, and we moved to a private dining room. I was now sitting with seven Fortune 250 CIOs! I asked them for advice. Although they couldn't relate specifically to the challenge of the EHR, they had significant experience in other transformative enterprise projects, such as ERP (enterprise resource planning). I wanted and needed to learn from their experiences. Yes, experience is a decent teacher, but other people's *evaluated experience* is the best instructor of all. I had no margin, time, or grace to "learn on the job." Unbeknownst to them, I saw them as my lifeline.

The modest cost of that dinner delivered significant returns. I gleaned more that evening than I could have gotten from a library or endless webinars. I selectively applied their golden nuggets of wisdom and sidestepped the pitfalls inherent to enterprise projects. Their willingness to share fueled the launch of my organization and propelled my team down the track of success.

The relationships I formed that day are as important today as they were then. I recently met one of these peers, Tom Lucas of Sherwin-Williams, for breakfast before the Society of Information Management's annual national meeting. Just as I had years ago, I peppered him with questions, then listened and learned. I needed to talk with someone outside of healthcare, and Tom was happy to be there for me.

What I've learned is that the more I reach out, the more easily I achieve my goals.

I want my direct reports to have similar interactions with their non-healthcare peers. My team routinely collaborates with non-healthcare companies. This summer we met with the IT leadership team from Kimberly-Clark. That meeting was pretty amazing, at least for us. We shared strategies, challenges, ideas, and opportunities. We commiserated and consoled. I went into my learning mode, and asked questions and took notes throughout the day. I was absolutely humbled by their advice and insights. As a result of our interaction, we adopted many of their leading practices:

- Launching an internal mentoring program
- Deepening our mobile strategy and consumer centric apps
- Developing a more robust communications capability
- Optimizing business intelligence

I was schooled and happy for it. But I admit remorse because I think we received more than we gave.

The secondary benefits of these interactions continue and we have now expanded our network to three non-healthcare companies. The members of my team have become genuinely acquainted with their peers in these organizations. They are now friends who can be called on to give them fresh perspective and whose insights help elevate my team's capabilities and performance.

Healthcare IT lags behind other industries like financial services, entertainment, logistics and retail. Networking with such organizations is one way we are closing that gap.

What I've learned: Reaching out transforms weaknesses into strengths.

What are your approaches for identifying and closing your technology gaps? Find a company you admire and reach out.

MEET THE PARENTS: MAKING LASTING FIRST IMPRESSIONS

Recently, I had the honor of getting to know the newest member of my team. Having been the newbie on the block, I know how awkward it can be. I was reminded of another newbie situation that happened more than two decades ago.

My freshman year had just ended and I was smitten. But Army Combat Medic School separated me from my college crush, making my summer unbearable. I didn't see Julie for twelve long weeks. Testosterone raging, I wanted to marry her. Right then! When I returned in that fall, our courtship blossomed. We started making plans for the rest of our lives and set a wedding date eighteen months out.

By then it was time to meet the parents.

A friend loaned me her Jeep over winter break. I drove my future bride through the ice and snow of Colorado to introduce her to my parents. Making our way from Ft. Collins south to Colorado Springs, we chatted about family as Julie played with the handcuffs that were mysteriously hanging from the rear-view mirror. She inadvertently cuffed herself. Laughing, we searched the Jeep for the key. No key.

I had no contact information for my friend, the owner of the handcuffs, who had gone to Florida for Christmas. Bouncing down I-25, Julie's arm dangled from the mirror. Refusing to let her meet my parents in this condition, I pulled into a truck stop and explained our dilemma to a repairman. Smirking up a storm, he cut the chain, freeing Julie's arm from the mirror. We continued our journey south.

We didn't want Julie's first introduction to my parents to include sawed off handcuffs, so we stopped at the Colorado Springs police headquarters where we requested assistance in removing the cuff. A suspicious desk sergeant pummeled her with questions. "Who did this to you?" Then he asked for the Jeep registration. It turned out the Florida vehicle had no registration. I started to consider my one phone call. "Dad, can you and Mom meet us at the police station and post bail?" Not the ideal first impression.

The cops finally released my future wife and me. Unable to de-cuff Julie, they sent us to a locksmith. After hearing our story, the locksmith called the cops and we repeated the cycle. Finally, after getting police clearance, the locksmith freed Julie. Although late, we reached my parent's home sans the inappropriate jewelry. Julie made an incredible first impression, and Mom and Dad immediately embraced her as part of the family.

I sometimes wonder if their reception would have changed if my fiancée had shown up with a sawed-off handcuff dangling from one wrist. It would have been a tough impression to recover from, for sure. Perhaps my parents would have attempted to bribe me as Julie's parents had tried to do, but that's another story.

You only have one chance to make a first impression, so make it good. The best thing about starting in a new organization is the opportunity to begin from scratch—with your management, your team and your customers. It's critical to think about the mechanics of that first impression long before you shake hands.

Great books such as *The First 90 Days*, by Michael D. Watkins, provide superb guidance. The best takeaway for me was not to "hit the ground running," but to "hit the ground listening." In my current position, I'd spent my first ninety days meeting with one-hundred key leaders, team members, and customers, taking copious notes all the while. I used these notes to guide my priorities that first year. The greatest gift we can give is to listen.

First impressions cut both ways and that is too easily forgotten when new employees, leaders, or customers come onboard. Go out of your way to make a positive impression on the new team member who clearly feels lost and out of place. Newcomers to any organization afford us with golden opportunities to show we care about their success. When possible, secure their contact information prior to their arrival and reach out in advance with an invite to dinner or coffee. In my role overseeing technology, I try to guarantee organizational newbies have all the tools and access they need to be productive on day one.

A first impression is more than personal. It's professional.

5
EMBRACE HUMILITY AND SERVICE

hum • ble (hum'bəl), adj.
1. not proud or arrogant; modest: to be humble although successful. 2. having a feeling of insignificance, inferiority, subservience: In the presence of so many world famous writers, I felt humble.

There is nothing like service to remind you that you are but a small part of a much bigger world. I have a picture that I use when I speak about humility—it's a picture of Jesus washing the feet of his disciples. It's a powerful and informative image.

Service can save you from narcissism. Serving others is a pathway to humility. Never think so highly of yourself that you lose touch with who you are and the others around you. If you come to think your success is all because of you, you have a problem. Remember that pride comes before the fall.

I think most people would say that I am humble, but it's tough and a bit oxymoronic to say it about yourself. While you do have to be a somewhat of a narcissist to be a leader, there are always opportunities to be humble and to serve those around you.

I tell my people that my job is to make them successful. I know that if I make them successful I will be successful. I believe that my approach has spawned more successful CIOs in healthcare than anyone else's. I can't prove that, but I believe it to be true because seven of my former direct reports are now CIOs.

My job—IT—is a service job. We exist to serve others. I therefore seek to be humble in my dealings with others.

Humble does not mean weak. There is great power in humility. I try to serve others at all times. I may lose some battles in the short term by being humble, but over the long term I will always win.

Seek first to serve.

THANKFULNESS IN ACTION

One morning before we began our leadership meeting a colleague, a chief nursing officer with whom I rarely saw eye to eye, came rushing up to me me. Although smiling on the outside, I braced on the inside for the tornado I expected would hit. I extended my hand in greeting, but she went straight for a hug. Not knowing her intentions, I was left feeling apprehensive and suspicious.

She released her impromptu embrace. "Ed, you sent me a thank you card for my service in nursing and I was like *ho-hum*. But what caught me off guard is when I walked into the nurses' lounge on our [medical-surgical] unit. On our community board was another card you sent to one of our floor nurses for her recognition as well. I tracked her down and she was blown away that a non-nursing executive would take the time to acknowledge her contributions in this way. It meant a bunch to her, to me, and not to mention her peers who all saw the card."

I'm paperless and proud of it. I have no printer drivers installed in my workstation. You'll rarely find me with a notepad, and I am judgmental of people—particularly those in healthcare technology—who still rely on paper. But I make one major exception. I still handwrite thank you cards. I always travel with blank thank you cards, and I send out eight during the course of an average week. Why?

Thank you card sales have hit an all-time low. Sure, digital convenience has displaced some of the need for them, but I think the real reason goes deeper than that. I fear that it's a combination of laziness and lack of training. Growing up in the Marx household, we could not enjoy any gifts we had received without first writing a thank you card. This became second nature to us kids, and we have since passed this tradition down to our children. I hope they will do the same with theirs. No thank you cards, no gifts.

They make a difference. Since handwritten cards are increasingly rare, their impact is magnified ten-fold. People still love to get snail mail, especially if it is personalized. You can open a card and hang it in your office or place it on a desk. You can touch it, smell it, and hold it to your chest. And another benefit: thank you cards differentiate you from those who do not send them. When I interview candidates, I absolutely pay attention to which interviewee sends a card and which do not. That little bit of effort speaks volumes and differentiates candidates.

Handwritten thank you cards are a tangible manifestation of the word *care*. Recipients not only see that you care, but they feel the effort and time it takes to

64

make such a gesture.

What's the chief virtue of handwritten notes? They don't beg for a response as do email. You email a *thank you*, and the person feels obligated to reply—"Back at ya ☺!" Doesn't that defeat the purpose?

Thank you strategies:

- Always carry a supply of cards, and when you become aware of an act deserving of praise, whip one out. The five minutes you spend writing could bring a day's worth of happiness to someone.

- Write cards with your leadership team. This is a standing agenda item at our weekly meetings. There is always someone deserving of praise. (Not to mention that sending a thank you is leadership by example.)

- When you see or hear of someone who has received an honor, send a card. For instance, whenever a top 100 nurse list is published, I "thank you" all the nurses who work in my organization.

- After concluding a meeting in which someone went above and beyond, start writing.

- Each Friday, a task pops up on my schedule that says: "Give Thanks." I reflect on the week and decide who to thank.

Testimonials:

- A grumpy executive responded to a thank you card via email. "Thank you so much for the card. The timing was perfect. Had a real rough week. Made everything worthwhile."

- A physician sought me out. "I have never received a thank you card from administration…this has given me fresh perspective."

- I was doing rounds with nurses in one of our hospitals when one approached me during a break. "Oh you're Ed Marx? We've never met, but you sent me a card *two years ago* (emphasis mine) for working with your team on an order set. Thank you for noticing and sending the card."

- Staff routinely stop me in the halls to say thank you for the card, some with tears in their eyes.

- My first platoon sergeant, a tough Vietnam vet, said, "Lt. Marx, I was like *what the shit*, I am just doing my job…and then it hit me, leaders do the little extras. I just sent short notes to my squad leaders."

- I sent a note to a CEO thanking him for his leadership and for the privilege of serving with him. His response: "…Nobody ever sent me a thank you card for no specific reason other than to say thanks for leading."

I have a confession to make. I do store some paper—actually it's a pile of thank-you cards I've received over the years. I can't toss them. They carry such meaning. I'd wager it'll be the same for the people who will receive a card from you. They become an oasis in a desert of thankless tasks. Like salve on a wound or the bridge over a chasm. They can make our toils all worthwhile.

To whom are you thankful? Your staff, your boss, a peer? Take action. Grab a card now and share your thoughts with that person. If your handwriting sucks, don't worry, mine does, too. But no one has ever complained about it, and I doubt anyone ever cared.

CONNECTING WITH STAFF

Own up. Once you leave a staff position and move into management, you cease to add productive value. Staff is the engine that pulls the train. Management is overhead and owes their success to staff. In a well run organization staff comes first, management second.

Management exists to serve and enable staff.

I connect well with staff because I am not one to forget my roots. I started as a janitor in a clinic, an experience that sparked my career in healthcare. Later, after some god-awful assembly line jobs and a short but endless gig filling sandbags, I made a commitment to myself to move into management. My goal was to reinvent staff work to make it more meaningful and efficient. After my lousy experiences, I promised myself I would treat staff as I wished I had been treated. As I worked my way through management, I observed and took notes. Tucking away all the good things from that experience, new inspirations sprouted and I recommitted myself to my personal pledge to maintain my connections to staff.

Management that loses touch slides downward into mediocrity.

Even today, I observe my peers and other managers and look for the gems. I actively seek to relate and stay linked. The day I lose touch is the day I become managerially impotent.

Here are some of my best practices:

- **Major Life Events.** Be there. Remember that what matters is your presence, not presents.

- **Hands-On Visits.** Go experience their work environment. I spend significant time traveling to our various facilities and hanging out with staff. I fill in at the service desk. Email and texting are *false forms* of relationship building.

- **Drop In.** I drop in on various meetings unannounced and just listen, answering but not soliciting questions.

- **Personal Parties.** I am always looking for a reason to host a party, especially in our home. We host several annual parties as well as impromptu ones. On average we have about 200 staff and family join us in our home each year.

- **Other's Parties.** I love getting invited to department parties, and I make them a priority. Nothing makes you feel more free than taking off your suit and letting out the real you.

- **Unique Venues.** Not everyone feels comfortable coming to my house. So I've started setting up gatherings at local bars. We publish schedule to give plenty of advance notice.

- **Sports.** I lead triathlon teams, adventure race teams, and climb teams. They provide tremendous opportunities for staff to bond. Sometimes I mountain bike with staff. And while I don't golf, I drive a mean golf cart.

- **Open Door.** Staff can view my schedule and itinerary and drop in whenever I'm in, wherever that may be.

- **Meals.** When I have free time, I actually send offers to see if anyone wants to go to breakfast or lunch. Impromptu meals are a lot of fun.

- **Exercise.** We have spinning, stationary cycling and treadmill conference rooms, and I let staff know when I'm using one. They're welcome to put on a pair of tennis shoes and we talk while exercising indoors to avoid the one-hundred degree Texas weather. Now that's efficient multi-tasking!

- **Volunteer.** Our team volunteers together. We've served in food banks, Habitat for Humanity, and other various service-based organizations.

- **Town Halls.** We do these once or twice per year. A little stuffy for me, but I do them.

- **Department Meetings.** Whenever I'm invited, I'm there.

- **Social Media.** For sure I connect with any interested staff on Facebook, Twitter, etc.

- **Collaboration Tools.** I microblog daily to staff, talking about what I'm working on as well as sharing general, organizational news. Staff can reach out to me in numerous ways including instant messages, texting and Yam. Email if you must.

- **Book Studies.** We do these quarterly. Eight-week sessions, one hour each. Great team building.

- **Holidays.** My wife and I make a point of serving my service desk staff on Thanksgiving and Christmas. We cater in all the food and have a giant feast.

I love my staff. It is a privilege and an honor to serve them. They make things happen, and connecting is one way I can add value back to the system.

How do you connect with your staff?

PRESENCE, NOT PRESENTS

It was the Southern Colorado District Tennis Championships. Playing Pueblo West in the finals, my Mitchell High School doubles partner and I were in for a tough match. For the first time, we would face line judges, a referee, *and* a crowd. (Gulp!). The stands were full and the tiny stadium was lined with people. We hit a few warm-up balls and then came the call for player introductions. The crowd and cheerleaders went wild for Pueblo West. "Cool," I thought. The announcer then called out our school and names next.

The silence deafened me.

Finally, a small but authoritative voice called from outside the fences. "Go, Ed'vard! Go, Ed'vard! Go, Ed'vard!" Yep, my Mom, in her thick German accent, cheered us on—one lone fan among the hundreds watching. Out of respect to us, and to honor my mom, the entire crowd broke into applause. We felt the love.

Moms teach us something unique about leadership. But their lessons they teach us about how to relate to others often get lost between high school graduation and our first day in the corporate world. We somehow compartmentalize the advice our mothers give us and end up leaving our relationship-building skills outside when we go into work each day. Yet the relationship skills that make a family tight knit is also what makes a team tight and helps a platoon to fight.

The rules you live by at home are good rules no matter where you are.

1. The Burden of Visibility. Like it or not, visibility comes with leadership. Once you leave line staff and enter a position of authority, your profile changes and others see you differently. Your primary purpose is now to serve the team or platoon actually doing the work. Your time is no longer your time. Your calendar becomes your staff's calendar. A great leader learns to be unselfish—just like a mom.

2. The Tactic of Availability. How available are you? Your staff could tell you because they're the first to know when you're not available. Do you insist your agenda be met, or do you find time to fit into your staff's agenda? When is the last time someone popped into your office unannounced just to talk? How often do you spend time outside of work with staff? Do you know all your staff's names and which team they serve on? (That can be tough but think how rough your childhood would have been if your mom had kept forgetting your name!)

3. The Participation Act. (This requires prioritizing, rearranging your schedule, and good time management.) Take part in life events. Even ten minutes of your life can make a world of difference to staff. Join in the celebration of a new baby, a marriage, or graduation. When tragedy strikes a member of your staff, mourn with them. Visit sick staff at home or in the hospital. Think about what really matters in light of the long term and make the small sacrifices. If your mom is your role model in caring for your fellow man, then practice what she preached.

4. Engagement. The more a leader engages, the more impact they have on their department. Be real. Be transparent. Who wants to serve a stodgy, closed-minded, secretive leader? Probably nobody you'd want on your team. Think back to whose house you played at as a kid? Probably the home where there was a mom to bake cookies, offer good advice and not fuss over messes. If you've ever dreamed of making your organization the best place to work then *engage.*

Here's a true story. As a young officer in Vietnam, Colin knew his troops feared death in the brutal killing fields of the Viet Cong. He assured them he would share that risk with them. When hearing that one of his men had stepped on a land mine and lost his legs, he commandeered a helicopter and flew off to rescue this young soldier. At great risk to himself, he ran through a mine field and carried the injured man back to his chopper and on to safety. Colin had every right to stay at his command post and attend to other duties. He could have lectured his staff on the dangers of war. He could have left the soldier to die and then written a nice letter home to his family about his noble sacrifice for freedom. Instead, he stuck his neck out and put himself at risk. He served. Nobody ever questioned his commitment to his staff and in response to his leadership his troops fought harder.

Now think back to your mom. If, when you were little, you had stepped off the curb and into the path of a car, would your mother have watched from the sidewalk? Or would she have leapt into the street to save her baby? A true leader will sacrifice himself to protect those he is in charge of.

We recently had a tragedy involving one of our staff. I mourned the loss of this great person and cried with his family who had just lost their husband and daddy. But I also cried because of the outpouring of love and support I witnessed from staff and leaders. We had leaders attend the ceremony who were not in this person's chain of command, but showed up in support for him and for his family. They could have just written a check to the designated scholarship fund, but they also chose to be in attendance, to swell the numbers of those who came to offer condolences.

Presence, not presents.

Time trumps a check every time. Your presence adds value. You may feel you are in a rat race but that doesn't mean you can't make a pit stop for humanitarian reasons.

Reap the benefits. They are numerous. When staff know you care, their level of engagement will rise. You can rah-rah all you like at staff meetings or in blog posts, but staff will respond to your actions. Words are only echoes of actions taken.

Colin, the young officer who crossed a minefield to save a young soldier, would eventually lead the entire U.S. military as Chairman of the Joints Chief of Staff, and later became our Secretary of State. I have spent time with General Colin Powell, and I can assure you his calendar has always reflected his commitment to the people he serves.

Still remember that district tennis championship? My partner and I lost our championship match 6-2, 6-1. Mom could have just picked us up afterwards and then given me a gift or taken me out to dinner. But what spoke volumes to me was her taking the time out of her busy day to stand in the heat and watch me play tennis. Losing with my mom present meant more to me than winning in her absence. That is how much time together means to me. It means the same to your staff.

Presence, not presents makes a good leader into a great leader.

P.S. While you are attending your staff's life events, watch to see who shows up who *did not have to* be there. Take note of their names, because you've probably seeing an emerging leader—and maybe the person who will some day replace you when you leave or retire.

LEADERSHIP EQUATIONS

It was the chairman of the Emergency Medicine department at University Hospitals Case Medical Center on the phone. "Ed, this is Dr. Michelson, do you know what is going on in our emergency department right now?" He was so upset and his loud tone made me think I was on speakerphone. I could tell he was calling from our Pediatric Level1 Trauma Center. I politely ended the call. As a new CIO, I did not want to have impersonal relationships. I wanted to talk face to face and so I went to him.

And there he was: directing traffic and evaluating patients like a battlefield medic doing triage. One of our IT applications had failed and it was wreaking havoc on their process flow. While there I noticed that we could alleviate some of the cramped conditions by updating their technology. It only took a couple of hours to restore the application, but IT's work wasn't done. The next day we restructured to give back additional space to the ED. All it took was simple things like replacing monitors, PCs and printers with more modern and space-efficient units.

I received a call the next day from our Chief Medical Officer. "Ed, I heard what happened yesterday. Nice work. That is the first time a CIO ever did something like this. Left the comfort of the ivory tower and walked the walk." Soon the story went viral and the benefits of an "eye to eye" approach become clear. I coined the term "i2i" and encouraged its adoption by everyone in my IT division. I started to live it. I stopped handling serious matters by email or phone. I did presentations on i2i for other departments. I was maturing as a leader.

I also began to use i2i for crucial conversations. I began to confront others i2i. We had a physician executive who routinely abused anyone who he believed stood in his way. Because he produced results, his behavior was tolerated. After exhausting escalations with chain of command and human resources, I took matters into my own hands. Over coffee, I mustered my courage and laid it out in no uncertain terms to this senior officer. He tried to look away but we connected i2i. He hid behind his coffee cup but my message landed. That was the last time he abused my staff.

Being a leader and serving your staff means that sometimes you need to get in someone else's face to defend your people.

I received a call from the medical director of one of our newborn intensive care units (NICU). This NICU is consistently ranked in the top five across the nation. After several attempts to resolve some technical matters, she and her administrative staff had become rightly infuriated with IT. They had twenty mobile carts for their NICU but *only two were operational*. She told me that nurses and physicians would literally stand in line to update charts and enter orders while caring for the sickest of the sick.

I was growing angry listening to this—not *at* the medical director, but *for* her! I had seen this problem escalate over a couple of days but I thought IT had taken care of the problem. I told the medical director I would be right over. I called the service desk as I walked over and asked the manager and three technicians to meet me at the unit. I could not believe what I saw. All these beautiful, tiny babies needing care and, sure enough, nurses and physicians waiting in line to use the two mobile carts that worked.

The the halls were littered with unusable carts—it looked as if a tornado had passed through! I approached the medical director and you could see the tears in her eyes because she was so upset. The only thing I knew to do was to embrace her, and then we both cried. Frustration, anger, compassion. There was release. Someone cared. Now it was time to execute. I learned then and there that it was critical to meet "emotion for emotion," or "e4e."

My staff arrived and I had them go to the other floors to see if we could borrow carts from other units. Within thirty minutes we had ten working carts. Others were replaced or repaired within 48 hours. I returned to our IT offices and found my director and VP of operations still talking about what to do to resolve the situation. I replaced them.

i2i and e4e are part of my business philosophy now. While there is no formula for leadership, these IT-style acronyms remind us that at the end of the day, nothing demonstrates care and commitment like looking someone in the eye, weeping with those who weep, and laughing with those who laugh.

Technology is the easy stuff. You are not a leader because you know technology. A leader is there to serve.

THINK WITH YOUR HEART

Will it shatter the image you have of me to know I cry at work? It's true. Whenever I give a tour or visit staff on a floor, at some point I excuse myself and cry. I can't help it, especially after talking with skilled clinicians who demonstrate their empathy. Seeing patients overwhelms me, and makes me think about the sanctity of life. My heart swings between pain and compassion, between awe and thanks. And this all drives me to keep doing what I do.

I never want to forget that I'm here to serve those in their most vulnerable times, often in the most dire of circumstances. One benefit of no longer having an office is my increased time spent in our hospitals and on our patient floors. My weekly leadership meetings—when we meet in person—are often held at one of our medical centers.

Why do I make my team do this, you ask?

A few years back, I realized that what separated the top performers from the average worker was neither skill or experience but talent. Further analysis revealed compassion was the key talent. Top performers connected skills with compassion. They linked their hearts to their brains.

I had to help others understand that what they did daily affected a patient's life. But how? A motivational speech might stir their emotions for a day or two, and that wasn't good enough. I needed an approach that transcended intellectual understanding, a connection so strong that synapses would rewire and link their brains to their hearts and infect their souls forever.

This awareness has led me to employ several strategies. The single most effective one is our annual *Connections* program. This spring will mark my seventh year with *Connections*. The remarkable happens when you remove the physical barriers between clinicians and those who support them. When a programmer sees the impact of his code on a patient, his heart is changed. When a service desk agent sees the face of the physician she'd helped navigate through the electronic health record, her heart grows a size. Sympathy awakes in a data center engineer when he learns from a nurse that patient outcomes improve when technology is delivered without interruption. And an administrative assistant better understands the urgency of communication when she personally witnesses the life and death situations.

Their brains tap into their hearts.

Here's how we did it, and then I'll share the outcomes with you.

- Everyone must participate, especially *you,* the leader. (Given how easy it is to revert to insularity and become ingrown, I keep my *connections* fresh)

- Speak with your hospital leadership and identify points of contact.

- Develop a schedule and allow employees to choose according to their interest, such as ED, OR, Lab, Nursing, Pharmacy, etc.

- Spend a minimum of a half day with a clinician, a full day is optimal.

- Set up an interactive site so employees can post feedback on their experience.

- Follow up immediately on any items clinicians need help with.

- Send thank you notes to all clinicians involved.

- Repeat this process once a year.

Outcomes:

- Results are transformative:

  o "I must admit I hated this idea but did it because I had to. I have worked for the health system for twenty years and for the first time I realized we have patients. Of course I knew what we did as a hospital but really, this was incredibly impacting and I will never be the same."

  o "I am not the same today as yesterday."

  o "I volunteered to observe in the OB unit. With clinician and patient permission, I witnessed the birth of twin babies. I never realized all the behind the scenes coordination required and it opened my eyes to a whole new world."

- ○ "I never saw myself as part of the patient care process until now."

- ○ "My life is changed; I always wanted to be care giver but didn't like blood so chose a different path in technology. Now I tell people I am both."

- ○ "I run marathons. I was more exhausted shadowing a nurse today. I never knew."

- ○ "In one day I witnessed the joy of healing and the pain of death. I now see how critical IT is and why we need to be the best that we can be to support the front lines."

- ○ "I am a nurse and did not see why I had to take part in this program. After today, it was like I was hit by a ton of bricks! Wake up call! Thank you, thank you, thank you."

- The clinicians shadowed learn more about technology. They learn that IT cares and that they have an incredible support structure surrounding them. This revelation is almost as beneficial as the *Connections* themselves.

- Respect from operational leaders increases because they see that you care.

- While not scientifically validated, there appears to be an overall correlation between organizational outcomes and *Connections*.

- As *Connections* form, employee engagement rises and new talents are created and nurtured.

I love giving a great speech, handing out raises and bonuses. But evidence suggests motivational speeches and perks have fleeting influence on performance. In fact, some studies indicate that enthusiasm over a raise lasts only a couple of weeks. I speculate this is because money only engages the brain. Conversely, transforming how we think and view ourselves results in long-term benefits and makes us a new person.

Even the hardest of hearts and the most gifted intellectual will begin to view things differently. Once they've *connected.*

WHO ARE YOUR PEOPLE?

While working on my blog, I had every intention of not doing another Ironman-related post. But my attempts to post on matters more closely associated with healthcare IT just weren't exciting me. Many of you had e-mailed asking me about the Ironman Arizona race. Perhaps this is indulgent but I would like to share some lessons I gleaned from that extraordinary event in my life, discoveries I made that apply to both leadership and life.

Ironman competitions are not easy under any definition of the word. Through all of the stress of this competition I held on to my perspective by thinking about Ellen, the person for whom I had run this race. I had given her all my medals from the events leading up to Ironman with the hope that in some small way they would be an encouragement to her and to her family. Her daily battle against her illness inspired me.

Thursday: I pulled in a few days early to acclimate to Tempe and to finalize my preparations. Though it was a long haul from Dallas, I chose to travel by car so I could bring everything I wanted, while keeping an eye on my bike. Once they put your bike in the cargo hold of a plane, you don't know what's going to happen to it. **You can better guarantee success by having the right tools *and* by making sure they stay in optimal working condition.**

Friday/Saturday: No grand feat—whether it's a major race or going live with CPOE (Computerized Physician Order Entry)—is performed well if attempted alone. Surround yourself with people who lift you up. One of my employees, Don, stopped in my office a few weeks prior to the race to inform me that he had started running for the sole purpose of praying for me. He timed a run to coincide with the start of the Ironman. Another employee, Aaron, flew out after the race to help me drive back to Dallas. I welcomed their support.

My son Brandon, also an experienced triathlete, flew in from college that Friday to assist me with the final prep and to give me counsel. As a film major, he shot all aspects of the race—a potentially interesting YouTube feature to come! We attended the Iron Prayer event to connect with other like-minded athletes. My wife and daughter, whose support I consider invaluable, arrived the day before the race.

Race Day—Athlete #1345: I awoke at 3 a.m. to begin the nutrition phase. I consumed a few hundred calories then slept again. Re-awaking at 4:30 a.m., I mixed my drinks and headed down to the transition area. My son was filming and helped me carry the specialized bags of equipment. By 5:30 a.m., my body was marked and my bike tires were pumped one last time. I found a spot under a tree and lay down to rest for the next 45 minutes. **Appropriate preparation and planning can allow you time to rejuvenate while others around you are scrambling to meet the deadline.**

T-Minus 30 Minutes: Under the scrutiny of the camera, I changed into my wetsuit. After a final interview, I jumped into the lake with the other 2,299 Ironman competitors. Even though I dislike the swimming leg more than the other legs, I remained unusually calm, partially because I was fully prepared. When the cannon fired, I was physically, mentally and emotionally ready to race. **Proper preparation precedes proficient performance.** (Say that ten times…)

First Dedication: Sam. Climbing out of the water, I picked up my bike bag and ran into the transition tent. My first transition was dedicated to Sam, the young son of one of my employees who was diagnosed with cancer last autumn. I pulled out the handwritten card with his name on it and placed it on the ground before me. I prayed for him as I put on my bike gear. His fight to the finish line would far surpass mine.

112 Miles in 6+ Hours: The strong head winds and the 95°F weather were killing my expected biking pace like a defunct router on network uptime stats. Complaining wasn't going to change anything. I had to make the best of it. Persevere. Keep focused on the bigger picture. I loaded up on fluids and consumed 400 calories per hour, a total intake of 3,000 calories, partly to prepare for the marathon ahead. Combating an urge to keep rolling, I made myself stop and re-apply lotions to keep from chafing. This would pay off later. At mile 80—my last time up yet another wicked hill—one leg started to cramp, and I realized I had yet to urinate. I forced down more drinks and salt tabs and the cramps subsided. At last, the final fifteen miles were downhill and flat. Relief washed over me.

During the last lap, the cameraman passed me backwards on his motorcycle, which meant the Ironman leader was right behind me. I sped up a little so when the scene unfolded on TV, it would look like I was in second place! That lasted about three frames as the leader zipped by making me look like I was standing still.

Second Dedication: Pam. The transition from bike to run was dedicated to Pam, the wife of one of my employees, who had breast cancer. I placed her name card in front of me and prayed for her as I changed. Only the marathon to go and I would be an Ironman. But how many marathons treatments did Pam have left? My suffering paled in comparison. **Thanks for your strength, Pam and Sam.**

Dedicated Players: Ironman staff had trained an abundance of volunteers to assist at every stage. At the first transition, volunteers stripped me out of my wetsuit while others applied sun lotion before the bike ride. As I ran down the middle of the bike compound, someone was at the end waiting with my bike. When I returned to the transition area, one volunteer took my bike while another handed me my run bag. I was again rubbed down with sunscreen before the run. Planted along the run route were hundreds of signs created by families of competitors in support of their athlete. My family had made motivational signs to help focus me on my purpose for doing the Ironman. **Surround yourself with people dedicated to your success, positive people who will encourage you despite the circumstance. They will get you through the loneliness and pain of challenging times.**

Strength vs. Weakness: In training, I deliberately chose to concentrate on my strengths: bike and run. I had invested a combined total of 353 hours on these two events. Had I invested extra time on the swim, I might have gained five percent in overall time. By concentrating on my strengths, I gained an estimated twenty percent. Twenty years ago, I almost made the mistake of returning to school for a technical degree. Realizing my strength was in leadership, I opted to develop those skills instead, and it paid off. What I might have learned in technology would have already been lost—and outdated. **Don't misallocate precious resources by devoting precious time to weaknesses.**

First, Break The Rule: I violated a cardinal race rule, which warns you should never ingest anything during a race that you have not tried in practice, because it could make you sick. Following a fellow Ironman's suggestion—one that he declared had saved him on the run—I indulged in a flat Coke. The sugar-caffeine high juiced my battery. Picking up the tempo, I cruised along with renewed vigor. **Sometimes you've got to shake things up a bit and not do the same things over and over, especially when they are not working.**

The End: I remember spotting the 26-mile mark on the marathon, but the last few hundred yards were a blur. Roaring crowds lined the grandstands. Officials held out the Ironman finish ribbon, and I raised my hands in triumph and received my medal. It was over. I had held nothing back. There is no rush like that of a mission fully completed.

Even at that moment of triumph, my eyes were searching for my family. My wife and I cried as we hugged. While my son continued filming, I embraced my daughter. This had been a long journey of very early mornings and regular sacrifices—a journey that took over our bathroom and kitchen with a plethora of Ironman gear and foods.

What's Your Bigger Picture? At the far side of the greeting pen was Ellen, the person for whom I had run this race. Throughout training, I had focused my prayers on the cruel disease that had invaded her body. I desired that, through the providence of God, those prayers would improve Ellen's quality of life. I presented her with the Ironman finisher's medal, and we both put up brave fronts for the camera though tears were streaming down our faces. Ellen does an Ironman daily, especially on her chemo days.

As a leader, do you have a significant purpose? Or is it solely about the money and the new house? Put people first. Seek to serve. In health care, the Sams, Pams and Ellens are the ultimate endurance athletes running a race that nobody should ever have to run. We are there for them.

By the way, I did get the Ironman tattoo which was nearly as painful as the Ironman itself!

FACES: THE TOUGHEST ASPECT OF BEING A CIO

When I'm asked "what is the most challenging part of being a CIO?" several thoughts come to mind. Things like losing a data center when the electric grid went down in the northeast; personnel matters; having to provide champagne service and applications on a beer budget; bearing the weight of decision-making knowing patient lives are at risk; facing down angry physicians; a multi-million dollar project gone bad. While these situations were tough, they are not the toughest challenges we face.

I think back to Zarema, a woman on the staff interview panel when I came through Texas Health Resources as a candidate. While her peers tossed softball questions at me, she played fast pitch. I loved it! I respected her *glasnost* approach and assertiveness. A recent immigrant from Russia, Zarema spoke with a thick accent and held to cultural mannerisms that sometimes clashed with our health system's progressive environment. Nevertheless, as a tireless and productive employee, she evolved into the go-to person for our IT division.

Before I left that division and eventually became CIO, Zarema confided in me that she was ill. I stayed abreast of her condition. She was very private but over time she received my prayers and support. Then one day I got the call. Disease had stolen her life. I lost an exemplar employee. Despite being sick, she had demonstrated how to strive for excellence, for she never settled for less than 100 percent on her yearly review.

I still see your face, Zarema.

A couple of years later, our IS Division underwent an incredible transformation, and much of the progress was attributable to our Field Engineering team. We suffered "ticket tennis" issues, meaning service requests were being lobbed between internal teams while the customer's needs remained unmet. By combining the separate functional areas of Desktop Support, LAN Admin, and Network, we adopted a Field Engineering concept that encouraged and rewarded collaboration, resulting in higher velocity and customer satisfaction. Dale was one of our young field engineers and a solid performer. Outside of work, he engaged in another passion: his motorcycle. One morning, he was tragically killed while riding his motorcycle to work. The funeral was packed, with the majority of our field engineers joining me in attendance. Listening to them share words of support with the grieving family I gathered morsels of this man's passion and added them to my treasury on life.

I still see your face, Dale.

I recall "Bill," the husband of one of my direct reports, taking ill. After a few days in the hospital, his wife told me that he had tired of cafeteria food. (Imagine that!) My son and I snuck tastier cuisine past the nurse station then hung out for a little bit and prayed with him. His death devastated me, as he left behind an infant daughter and a young wife. He was brave; he fought hard. And he reminded me how life was too short to not live it abundantly.

I still see your face, Bill.

Most recently, another member of my division passed away suddenly. I regret, given my short tenure, that I did not have the time to get to know "Maggie." Co-workers shared that she was a dedicated employee and a wonderful person, someone I would have appreciated. During a moment of silence at an all-staff meeting, I studied this woman in a picture on PowerPoint. I imagined visiting her at her desk, and I wondered what wealth of character I might have gained from knowing her.

I still see your face, Maggie.

So what is the most challenging experience as CIO? It's empathizing with tragedies that befall my department: lives taken prematurely; the impact of death and disease on families and communities. A good leader will mourn with those who mourn and rejoice with those who rejoice.

I have attended many wakes and funerals to console grieving staff who lost children, parents, grandparents, spouses, and other loved ones. Some are still in my contacts and scheduled so that their birthdates and legacies chime annually on those bitter yet beautiful days.

I still see their faces.

MEMORIAL DAY: WHAT IS YOUR LEGACY?

In April 2007, while in Washington D.C. on business, I spent some time sightseeing with some fellow former Army officers. One gentleman was the recently retired commanding officer of the Third U.S. Infantry Regiment (Old Guard) charged with guarding Arlington Cemetery, including the Tomb of the Unknown Soldier. He gave us a most unexpected honor.

He prearranged for a couple of us to lay the flowered wreath at the Tomb of the Unknown Soldier during the evening changing of the guard. I still get chills as I reminisce about that moment: escorted between somber, armed soldiers; laying an inadequate garland of flowers before a tomb steeped in honor and tradition; silently saying "thank you" for unknown men who made the ultimate sacrifice, men we lost but have never forgotten. The sight of our flag coupled with the singing of our national anthem generally brings tears to my eyes. For me, this honor was as good as it gets.

A sacrifice... never forgotten. Despite language, religious, and geographical differences, humanity shares a universal desire: to make life meaningful. Whether it means having an impact on your family, village, or nation, we all want our lives to count for something.

The Memorial Day Service my wife and I attended this weekend reminded me of the brevity and sanctity of life. Every song sung, every speech read, each poem recited proved life is be lived with relevance and significance. Am I living in such a way that those who benefit from my work will take time to reflect on my contributions? For some, *contribution* means laying down life in battle to defend freedoms. For another, service and sacrifice will have a different flavor. Whatever we are called to do, let us impact people positively as we serve forthcoming generations.

I began to personalize these thoughts in terms of my career. "There's no limit to the amount of good you can do if you don't care who gets the credit." I don't know who said that, but it's a truism that helps me keep a healthy perspective. The world isn't about me, but it does either gain or suffer based on my involvement, how much I give and take.

My new philosophy goes like this:

Let my company be a better place for teaching, healing, and discovering as a result of my leadership. Let the decisions I make have lasting beneficial effect. May I treat others in such a way that their children and their children's children will benefit. May I always keep the long-term in mind so as to avoid compromise and complacency. Let me leave my company a better place than when I arrived. May those I serve accomplish more than otherwise possible, furthering their careers and thus their impact. May clinical and business outcomes be positively impacted and lives improved.

Though no one else may see it, my epitaph will read: *my service in healthcare mattered!*

What about you? Will yours be a legacy that is remembered?

6
FIND AND
FUEL PASSION

pas • sion (pash'ən), n.
1. any powerful or compelling feeling or emotion, as in love or hate. 2. a strong or extravagant fondness, enthusiasm or desire for anything: *a passion for music.*

You have to be passion driven. People can see the passion I have for my life—they constantly comment on it when I am speaking about leadership. You have to find what you are passionate about and continually fuel it.

Passion drives energy and commitment.

As CIO at my present organization, there is a phrase I use that encapsulates why I am so passionate about what I do: "we save lives." Regardless of what we do, whether it's IT or admin or facilities or as a nurse on the front line, our work leads to lives saved. We save lives. That's my mantra and it drives my passion for this work.

My family has this thing we do around the dinner table—it's called "highs and lows." Essentially we go around the table and talk about the worst and best things that happened to each of us that day. And even on the worst day, I can hold my head up and say that what I did that day saved lives. That's a powerful motivator, even when I am being taken to the wood shed over something.

It doesn't have to be about work. Passion should be a part of your entire life. Finding the thing or things you are passionate about can start outside your career. For example, my wife and I are passionate about the Argentine Tango.

How do you discover your passions? Live your life. Try new things. Take risks. Ask yourself open ended, reflective questions. If something moves you emotionally, pay attention to it. You have to let life affect you to find what drives your passion.

BANK LIFE, NOT VACATION DAYS.

If your organization is like mine, you are fairly data driven. We have Key Performance Indicators (KPI) to track business and clinical metrics that help ensure we're headed down the right path. Our published dashboards let employees and the public know how we are doing in fulfilling our vision and mission. We use the data, drill down as needed, make adjustments, refine processes, improve and continue forward. There is a reason why data-driven organizations outperform those that are not.

I have drawn these analogies before. If it works so well in business, why don't we apply the same principles to what matters most—life? So I pondered this…

What would the KPIs be for my life? One that jumps to mind is the balance on my Paid Time Off (PTO) account. A high balance warns of danger while a low balance indicates just that—balance.

Confession time. I used to pride myself on statements like "I am too busy to take PTO" or "my role does not allow me to take much time off." Poppycock!

When I switched jobs, I enjoyed "cashing in" the 600-hour balances I maintained. But at what cost? My family and my well-being!

Never again.

Listen to me. I am not waiting until retirement nirvana to spend time with those I love. I may not make it there. And if I do, my "loved ones" may no longer recognize me.

So this year I started taking more time off with the goal of maintaining a PTO balance below 100 hours. And taking time off does not necessarily mean spending money and traveling to Timbuktu. It can mean just staying at home or volunteering at a local service organization. There are numerous organizations that need us.

The benefits to routinely spending your hard-earned PTO are numerous. First and foremost is your personal well-being. Ample evidence shows a direct correlation between well-being and happiness. You must take care of yourself so you can help take care of others. When you do this, your family wins, society wins. Gallup research shows that by increasing well-being you also increase productivity. The more you rest, the more restored you become, the more effective you are at work. We have all seen the ragged co-worker who never takes PTO, working sixty-hour weeks. In most cases, when productivity and well-being are sapped, a person becomes impotent.

Been there, done that. Not going back.

Bringing it squarely back to work, think of the benefit to your team. Counterintuitive perhaps? When you're gone, a couple things happen. One, they get a much needed break from you. True that! Everyone needs a break from their manager now and again. Nobody is that good, or indispensable. Two, it demonstrates trust in a way words cannot. I recently took PTO, and my staff had to lead and deal with two major events without me. You know what? They did not miss me. In fact, one could argue they did better because I wasn't there!

Admittedly, I still struggle to unplug once I am off. I have a great team at the office and my worries are few, but I struggle to break my work addiction. That may drive another KPI.

Take your PTO. You earned it. I don't give a flip what your role is or what projects are coming up. You are not that important. Certainly not more important than what your family needs: you. You in the moment. You rested. You there.

Get your rear out of the office.

CONFESSIONS OF A REFORMED MULTITASKER

I was wrong. Multitasking is not only overrated, it's *the* thief of our times.

New Year's Eve 2008, on a plane en route to our Marx Family Annual Strategic Planning Retreat, I read *Chasing Daylight*. The author, Eugene O'Kelly, was the CEO and Chairman of KPMG. At 53, he was diagnosed with a terminal brain tumor. He quit his job to settle accounts with friends and family and wrote a book to convey what he learned through the experiences of life and death. Based on the principles espoused in his book, I added the following to my personal strategic plan:

- Live in the Moment

- Energy > Time

- Consciousness > Commitment

- Create Perfect Moments

The above principles originated from research done by the Human Performance Institute. I attended their "Corporate Athlete" training where these concepts and related evidence-based theories took on renewed meaning. I was confronted with the truth on multitasking. The idea of energy management struck me. **The Bottom Line:** If you desire high performance, then don't multitask. Avoid a multitasking lifestyle if you care about the personal message you are sending people. Gulp. Seriously? Guilty!

It had to start at home. Almost every evening, I'm home for dinner by 6 p.m.—a sacred time. But now: no Blackberry, no checking messages, no calls, no social media and no vendor meetings. My energy and focus are on my family. Love is a verb, and I show my love by giving them my undivided attention. Emotional energy is a relational factor that surpasses time. I don't tell them, I *show* them that they are more important than my vocation.

In fact, the stronger my family relationship, the stronger I am as an employee. I find that leading others is a rewarding honor, and by definition, a CIO must give energy to those he serves. I have stopped multitasking where face-to-face encounters are involved. I still multitask but never when I'm with people. What message does it send to them when I'm not fully engaged?

Has your manager ever multitasked while you share your ideas or answer a question? How did it make you feel? Have you had to repeat questions or respond to duplicate inquiries as a result of someone multitasking? How about during conference calls when you call on someone only to get silence…and their phone isn't on mute (guilty). I wonder how many people I have inadvertently frustrated by having to revisit subjects previously discussed because I'd been trying to juggle tweeting, emailing, and preparing a presentation. Was I genuinely *in* the meeting to begin with? After observing a leadership meeting, one of my favorite doctors admonished the group for focusing more on email than on the discussion. Kudos to him! How much productivity had been lost?

I am a huge advocate of technology and displacing paper and paper-based processes with automation, but we must exercise balance. Use your iPads, mobiles, tablets and laptops to conduct business but be disciplined and remain focused on the subject and people, not your email or twitter feeds. Make time for that later.

For those who still believe they can effectively multitask while still giving appropriate attention to family and staff, a Google search will reveal numerous scientific studies to support my thesis that high performance and multitasking are mutually exclusive. In fact, Stanford University researchers found that multitasking may degrade our ability to think clearly and separate relevance from irrelevance, all while degrading memory/learning. They conclude by saying "by doing less, you might accomplish more."

The way I spend my time and invest my energy reveals what I believe most deeply.

HEALTHCARE PASSION REFUELED

My passion for healthcare sprouted in high school while working in environmental services at an outpatient facility. Back in the '80s they called us *janitors*. From that point forward, different encounters have renewed that passion. The most dramatic experience was personal.

A Journey Home. Three years ago this month, my mom traded her earthly rags for a robe of righteousness. After a courageous four-year fight against the ravages of ovarian cancer, Ida Wilhelmine Marx bid us farewell. The entire experience had a profound impact on me not only as a son but also in my profession.

My mom and I were tight. As I blindly plodded my way through adolescence, she represented mercy and grace. When I shoplifted, got arrested for joy riding (14 years old), set the house on fire, partied excessively, and flunked junior high, she was there. I'm convinced that if it weren't for my mother's care balancing my father's discipline, I would not enjoy the successes I have had in my education, career, and family.

Radiance. Mom suffered from illnesses her entire life. She took the cancer in stride: eight rounds of chemo, two rounds of radiation and a couple of surgeries. Her sole desire before transitioning from this life to the next was to celebrate her 50th wedding anniversary. When we transferred her to hospice, it became apparent that she would be a few weeks shy of reaching her goal. With my parents' permission, my brothers and sisters planned an early 50th anniversary party and vow renewal—the final celebration of mom's life. Knowing our world would change the following day, that night we put on a heck of a celebration.

Hollywood could not have written a better script. Hospice physicians agreed to give my mom life-sustaining nutrients and fluids through the big day (normally not allowed). They arranged for a "Sentimental Journey" pass: a limousine (ambulance) service for my mom and dad to the picturesque Cheyenne Mountain Resort in Colorado. Two paramedics waited in the background just in case their services were needed (they weren't). They quipped how special my mom was because the only other person who ever received two paramedics as an escort was former Vice President Dick Cheney when he came to town.

All seven of us children attended plus all fifteen grandchildren. My parents invited their closest friends. With the backdrop of the Rockies and all the majesty of a traditional wedding ceremony, I had the privilege of walking my father to the front. My oldest brother, Mike, had the honor of escorting my mom in her wheelchair to join my dad at the altar. She looked ravishing: my sisters had dressed her to the "nines." Her dream was unfolding in real time.

Each of her children had a part in the ceremony as did each grandchild. Assigned to deliver the sermon, I decided not to use notes but instead prayed that God would intervene and deliver a message that would bless my parents and set a vision for successive generations. The primary message: my parents had created a legacy of marriage that would impact not only the first generation (me and my siblings), but their grandchildren, and their grandchildren's grandchildren, and so forth. The fact that my parents stuck it out and endured a lifetime full of sickness and health is a testimony to the world: "Yes, it can be done."

The ceremony ended with the exchanging of vows. A co-worker of mine had arranged for a Papal blessing of the 50th milestone as well, which touched my parents deeply. We printed the blessing in the renewal program. Unity candles, songs, prayers, and standing ovations lent to the evening's incredibleness. But this was only the beginning.

One Heck of a Show. We then entered the adjoining room for a superb five-course meal. Taking advantage of the live music and dance floor, dad rolled mom out in her wheelchair to dance. My parents are fantastic dancers, and seeing my dad wheel my mom around was moving. Throughout dinner and beyond, we danced to our hearts' desires. All four sons danced with mom, who was clearly delighted. Even my son, Brandon, danced with her, about whom she commented: "You're not dancing. You're just shaking your ass!" Next were the toasts and the garter ceremony, and all the similar accruements of a fine celebration. At that point, mom addressed the room with loving words. Dad tried but fell apart. As a finale, guests and family formed a tunnel by joining hands. Dad wheeled mom through as we hugged, kissed, cried, and spoke blessings. Returning to her limousine, she was still beaming. My dad shared that as he laid mom in her bed that evening, she said, "We sure gave them one hell of a show tonight, didn't we?"

Timing. During her illness, I flew out often to visit her. I wanted to be at her side when she transitioned, just as she had been at my side so many times. I missed by eight hours. But that was okay. Over the years, I'd left no doubt in my mother's heart of my care, admiration, appreciation, and love for her. Arriving shortly after her passing, I supported my brokenhearted father and assisted with the funeral arrangements.

Kiss. My mom had taken her last breath shortly after midnight. Two of my siblings and my father were at her bedside and described that, while painless, her body struggled for every last breath. As a result, her mouth was stuck wide open. The hospice nurse explained that, given the timing, the mortician would be the only one able to close Mom's mouth. My sister-in-law, an ICU nurse manager, validated this.

Meanwhile, my dad knelt at mom's bedside and held her frail body, the first time in months where he could hold her without causing her pain. He kissed her lips. Wept over her. Sometime in the next two hours, while they awaited the mortician's arrival, mom's mouth closed…and she smiled. Comfort permeated the room and reinforced our belief that she had indeed transitioned to a happier place.

Passion Fueled. My mom's battle allowed me to spend considerable time in various care settings. I observed the processes, evaluated technology, and pondered how things could be improved to benefit caregiver, family, and patient. The clinicians treating my mom lacked the communications and clinical decision support needed to deliver the highest quality of care. I was shocked by the lack of access to critical and timely clinical data. The wasteful amount of paper utilized and manual processing disappointed me. I swore it would never be this way in my work environment. As I took mental notes from the perspective of patient and family, my passion to leverage technology and transform the clinician and patient experience was renewed.

It's *this* passion that drives me in my daily work. This is why I'm tenacious in advocating technology, why I continually innovate and collaborate with clinicians, and why I blog. This is why I advocate for more *meaningful* meaningful use. It's the heartbeat behind why I spend more time with my people on leadership, customer service, process, and passion than I do on bits and bytes. Until my people have a heart for patients and are in a position to empathize with their plight, the bits and bytes will be limited. The full potential of technology in the delivery of high quality healthcare comes with a transformed heart.

Thanks, mom, for refueling my passion as a leader of healthcare technology.

GREEN TIME

In just the last few years, the Green movement has picked up momentum as the world comes to grips with the reality that we belong to a single ecosystem and must be prudent caretakers of our shared Earth. Sidestepping the political foray associated with the movement, one principle I agree with is conserving our precious resources. The most precious non-renewable resource of all is our time. I advocate "Green Time."

My audiences and blog subscribers often ask how I manage to accommodate all my passions—and still do them well. After a recent talk on mentoring a woman said to me, "I have read your blogs and seen your YouTube Ironman videos where you share the amount of hours invested in training. If you were to take a twenty-week period and subtract the time for training, sleeping and working, how do you have time for anything else?" She stated the exact hours associated with each.

Part of the answer boils down to personality where my wife will attest to my unconventional modus operandi. Aside from that, however, I do not subscribe to the work-life balance philosophies popular over the past decades. Technology has created the capacity for more fluidity and integration in the post-modern lifestyle, freeing us from the bounds of compartmentalization. If I am inspired at 3 a.m. to work on something, or on a Saturday, so be it. If I want to be home for an important mid-day occasion, I do it. I measure my productivity in outcomes, not hours.

There are numerous books on time management that will do a far better job than I in providing tools and tips, but here are a few tips that work for me.

- Team Work Makes the Dream Work

  - You are only as successful as the people around you.

  - You must have a great assistant like I do.

  - Delegate authority and responsibility to the lowest levels possible.

  - Provide vision and remove barriers, then get out of the way and allow your team to make it happen.

- Multi-Task

  - I carry out the majority of my conference calls while in the car. (Safety tip: integrate a complete Bluetooth environment in your car to do this.)

  - My laptop with "aircard" shadows me everywhere enabling

me to catch-up on miscellaneous tasks during any unexpected downtime.

- ○ I keep up *intake* (reading, studying) while biking and running indoors.

- ○ All division leadership meetings include 29 minutes for professional development.

- ○ Outdoor runs, rides, and swimming incorporate prayer and reflective thinking; Blackberries are great for spontaneous note taking.

- Meetings

  - ○ I attend fewer meetings by allowing others to represent me.

  - ○ Too often, I have looked around a meeting room at the people involved and wondered at the duplication of effort and wasted resources.

  - ○ I always ask myself, "Was my attendance really necessary?"

  - ○ I adopted principles from the book *Death by Meeting*, by Patrick Lencioni, and improved outcomes.

  - ○ I create regularly scheduled "block times" where I do not attend meetings.

  - ○ Practice those things you probably know but don't do: agenda, meeting purpose, facilitator, timekeeper, action items, etc.

- Stop Watching TV

  - ○ The average person watches somewhere around 20 hours per week. Set yourself free, and buy back 20 hours!

  - ○ I married my college sweetheart between our junior and senior years. Possessing little cash, we lived without a TV and never became addicted. Today, we watch a couple of movies per month and enjoy an exceptional TV moment such as the Olympics. Even then, one of us will climb on the elliptical or stationary bike instead of acting the couch potato.

- Vendors
  - o I only spend time with strategic partners; my team handles tactical and emerging partners.
  - o I rarely do lunch or dinner meetings or other boondoggles. Instead, I do occasional breakfast meetings, which are quick and part of my existing work routine.
  - o I've started doing workout meetings. We meet at the gym and talk while working out.
- Work from Home
  - o I save up many routine and/or intensive tasks for my home workday, Fridays. My productivity easily increases by fifty percent or higher. My assistant does this as well. My entire division is encouraged and free to work at home as much as possible.
  - o If the above is impractical, carve out a minimum weekly four-hour block of time and visit your neighborhood Starbucks, Barnes & Noble, Panera, library, etc. Free yourself from distraction, and concentrate on work for an extended period of time.
- Be mission and vision driven, and take control of your destiny
- Focus
  - o Where ever I am and whatever I do, I am in the moment.
  - o I begin each workday by seeking God and preparing for the day's and week's tasks and objectives.

- ○ I give everything I have to the task at hand.

- Outsource

  - ○ I hire others to do tasks that sap my energy and time, such as lawn care and household/car repairs. Some say they can't afford this. I argue you can't afford not to if you want to have energy to focus on what will help you realize your vision.

  - ○ "Outsource" other home tasks. Teach your children certain tasks. (Our son received his A+ certification training at age 12; for six years he was the household go-to person for all things technical.) The neighbors hired him on several occasions for computer needs. Do your neighbor kids have skills you can employ?

- Exercise

  - ○ Studies have shown that exercise not only improves the odds of a longer more healthful life, but sharpens the mind.

  - ○ I do the majority of my workouts while others are sleeping. My workout facility opens at 5 a.m. and is five minutes from my office. Time and location are significant conveniences.

  - ○ Golf! I've never stepped foot on a course, but many CIOs do. Are you using those three to four hours wisely? Can you golf with family or with vendors?

- Family time

  - ○ Evening walks. Weekend bike rides.

  - ○ Got teenagers? We connect with ours by playing Rock Band. (Although I am the lead vocal, my kids have warned me not to quit my day job).

  - ○ My kids let me practice my speeches on them and use them as sounding boards. They get a taste of what I do, which keeps us connected and broadens their perspectives.

- o Part of my weekly dates with my wife include a joint work-out and prayer, things we both believe in.
- o Regular dates with the kids are crucial.
- o Family first + work second = everybody happy.

- Rest and the Sabbath

  - o I get to bed around 9 p.m. each evening for an average of seven hours sleep per weeknight, more on the weekends.
  - o I attempt to reserve Sundays for pure rest, no work of any kind. Counterintuitively, this principle when applied leads to more time abundance.

- Mood affects everything

  - o Gratefulness allows me to enjoy the time I do have.
  - o Always give thanks. I was a janitor and I was thankful. I was a pizza delivery driver and I was thankful. I was an Army private and was thankful. I am a CIO and am thankful. In all things, give thanks. It's a choice.

I don't believe our environment is completely controlled by the actions of the population, but I do know I'm responsible for how I manage my personal time. Hence, my choices govern my impact on those around me.

In this sense, I'm a dogged proponent of "Green Time."

LIVE THE MOMENT.

Oh, we were so very young. Married at twenty, our first child, Brandon, was born shortly after our college graduation. As the first of our friends to have a child, we were novices. My wife Julie became the primary caregiver while I worked full-time and completed graduate school.

When Brandon was six months old we started "dating." Saturday mornings became father and son bonding time, giving mom a break. He was able to sit up, which meant he could hold his own seat at the Dunkin Donuts counter where we indulged in baskets full of munchkins and memory-making. We spent anywhere from two to four hours together each Saturday, and as he grew, our dates became more sophisticated—but they always included breakfast out.

Over time we incorporated walks, feeding ducks, workouts, praying, and board games. We discussed everything from sports to toys to friends to girls and, more recently, college and women! Nineteen years later—over 975 dates—we calculated that we had clocked 4,000 hours of one-on-one time. Man, I have relished each moment. When I dropped him off at Biola University in Southern California, I was so happy to have had those precious times together. Even so I still wept as I drove away.

I determined many years ago to live life without regret. I sought out and discovered my purpose and have since organized my life around that one rule. Out of this grew my decision to live in the moment. Yes, I study the past to learn from experience, and I have a vision for the future to direct me; but I aim to maximize each moment and be truly alive.

Sometimes this means just sitting back for a couple of minutes and breathing. I mean *real* breathing, deep and reflective, if you will. We spend so much time beating ourselves up over the past and worrying about future troubles that we lose out on the important stuff of today. We must choose to live in the present.

I share all this because we have made significant accomplishments at organizations where I have had the privilege to have served, and I am sure you have done the same. As leaders we must always make the time to celebrate and enjoy. But not in ways that make us complacent. May it never be! We must continue to push for improvements and progress, balanced by regular self-examination.

Depending on where I am and who I am with, I try to reflect regularly. Occasionally, I do this with my team. "Lets take a second and look around the room. Each of us has played a key role in the success of this organization. This is a unique moment in time. We won't always be together as a team. Life happens.

Careers compel us forward. Enjoy one another and this moment."

Throughout my Army and healthcare careers, I have had the privilege of being a part of many special teams. Even as I write this, I can recall "moments" with each organization, and I can picture the people around me. We accomplished objectives of value but rarely at the cost of a time unexamined or a person unappreciated.

The day will come when each of us will leave our current organizations, ideally with a worthy legacy. While we are here, let us continue to be excellent stewards of our responsibilities. While we learn from the past and embrace the future, let us not forget to live in the moment. Oscar Wilde said it well, "To live is the rarest thing in the world. Most people exist, that is it." Live the moments you have, it is a decision you will never regret.

P.S. The dating ritual with Brandon influenced my decision to do the same with my daughter, Talitha, beginning shortly after her birth. We are at 650 dates and counting. Although my wife and I have maintained a consistent dating relationship, we've lost count of the number. Oh, and somewhere along the way we moved from donut holes to healthier fare…except on special occasions!

MY JOURNEY TO CIO

As a 16-year-old sanitation engineer (they called us janitors back in the 1980s) working the evening shift at the 21st Medical Group Clinic at Peterson Air Force Base, I never envisioned myself having a healthcare career. I was more concerned about adjusting the volume on my new Sony Walkman than I was with how dirty the floor looked. That is, until I met Tech Sergeant Samuelson. Samuelson worked in the ED (Emergency Department) where I signed in and out each shift. He loved his job and it showed in his smile. He had a passion that I did not. Unknowingly, Samuelson seeded my vision to serve in a profession where I could impact the lives of people, much as he impacted mine.

The summer prior to college, I enlisted in the Army Reserves and became a Combat Medic. Although I had limited opportunity to serve others in an actual crisis, I relished the time I spent training soldiers for the worst. It was more than a job. As my university studies progressed, I left the medical corps to be commissioned as a Combat Engineer Officer. I enjoyed the challenge, but I missed giving shots and driving an ambulance. In a job that appeared to be a divergent footnote to my graduate studies, I gained an appreciation for technology and its ability to enhance processes and enable transformation. Consider it another experience pouring still more of the foundation on which my future would be built. The question was, how would my passion for healthcare meld with my emerging interest in technology?

As providence guided, I landed a position at a community hospital as an Anesthesia Aide. I had applied for dozens of senior positions, but because of my relative lack of experience I couldn't get interviews. As an Anesthesia Aide, I honed my clinical experience and learned more about patient care processes. That experience was key to my future. I developed relationships with clinicians and administrators and was eventually offered a position in administration. Unlike the traditional CIO, I rose up through the business ranks while attaining both clinical and technology experience. In leveraging these three divergent disciplines, I discovered my niche but, moreover, I allowed my vision and passion to move me forward into my calling.

My career soared and afforded me many cherished memories of institutions and people. I have served as a leader in academia, single hospitals and IDNs (Integrated Data Networks), in for-profit and not-for-profit environments—the last five years as a CIO. But what stokes my fire each day is knowing in my heart of hearts that what we do as professionals in healthcare information technology has a significant impact on those whom we serve, our patients.

7
PERSEVERANCE
AND RESILIENCY

per • se • ve • rance (per'sə'ver'əns), n.
1. doggedness, steadfastness; resolute and unyielding
holding on in following a course of action in sprite of
difficulties: *Endurance and perseverance combined to
win in the end.*

Life is hard and unfair and bad things happen even to good people. They key is to persevere.

It is often in the valleys, when things appear most bleak, that rebirth can occur and, if momentum is maintained, we can come out stronger and wiser on the other side. Resiliency enables you to bounce back. Winners are often those who kept going after hitting a wall. A loser is someone who hits that same wall, but doesn't get up.

Perseverance is key—people tend to give up to early and they miss their chance at having extraordinary experiences. Whether it's an IT challenge or a triathlon or a mountain climb, there is always a point at which I just want to give up and quit. *It's too hard.* But, I have learned that quitting is the one thing you never do.

Sometimes perseverance is about outlasting your opponent. When I was in my thirties, I was playing tennis in a tournament called the Paper Cup in Colorado. I had to battle my way through difficult matches and by the end of the day I was completely spent. When I woke up the next morning to prepare for the finals later that day, I could barely move my upper body or walk. I didn't know what to do. I felt like I couldn't play and that I should drop out of the tournament. It was really bad. But I went ahead anyway and as it turned out, it was my opponent who dropped out and defaulted. Had I given up, I would not have won.

I learned perseverance from my parents. They endured and made the best of their lives even during the worst of times.

When I was seventeen, I had no money, no friends and a 1.6 GPA. I felt like my life was coming apart around me. Part of me just wanted to throw in the towel and give up. But somewhere inside me, I knew that if I stuck it out and kept pushing I would eventually make it; things would eventually get better.

A lot of people settle for second best. Don't be one of them. Outlast. Be tenacious. Persevere.

ELEVATION: PREPARING TO RISE

Leaders elevate to reach summits. As the slope rises, so must leadership.

I soaked in the view from six peaks over fourteen months. Some were well marked, long trails that were more hike than climb (Pikes Peak, 26 miles). Some stood tall, surpassing 19,000 feet (Kilimanjaro), and others involved steep alpine terrain that required technical equipment (Rainier). Each one spawned cherished memories and required a bit of bravado. But here is the truth. In every one of those climbs, there came a point when I wanted to quit.

At the start of each ascent I have a good attitude, I am ready to lead teams to the top. Easy street! Gear is not an issue and my body is fueled and rested. The terrain is normally flat and the weather agreeable. But invariably the pitch steepens and the pace slows. Breathing becomes intentional, and team chatter dissi-

Having some downtime with my "partner in climb", Dr. Liz Ransom, who serves as my climbing expeditions co-lead and medical director. Mt. Elbrus Base Camp, July 2013

pates. Enthusiasm wanes as fatigue sets in. Uncontrollable variables heighten the challenge. Snow, rain, wind, and freezing temperatures penetrate your clothes. Covered crevasses, possible avalanches, and wildlife prey on your senses. Equipment failures attack when you least expect it. And when you need strength the most, you find don't feel like eating or drinking. Negative self-talk creeps in. If no one ever found out, you'd stop and turn back.

We left the Muir base camp at Mt. Rainier just after midnight. We awoke to howling winds blowing ice and sand in our faces. We immediately put on ski masks and added insulating layers. Despite fresh batteries, my head lamp failed. This was going to be one tough climb to the top of Rainier. That is how we began. After crossing the Muir snowfield, we had our first break at 2 a.m. I was already thinking, *what the heck did I get myself into?* Guides checked on their teams and warned that the most difficult sections were still to come. Some turned back to Muir. If I turned back, would my team give up as well? If I continued without inspiration, would I put my team in danger?

My unwritten covenant for leading people: To be the leader I aspire to be, I must elevate to match the slope before me.

Settle the mental gymnastics before you even get in such a situation. That's what saved me on Rainier's *Disappointment Cleaver*. When I become discouraged, I fall back on the truth. It is imperative that leaders have bedrock beneath them for times such as these. Climbing mountains figuratively or literally requires self-assurance. Here are some techniques to ensure truth and sure footing when your toenails turn black and your feet become sore and blistered.

- **You will rise to your level of training.** Conquer smaller mountains in preparation for the bigger ones. Listen intently to your instructors and learn how to self- and team-arrest in the event of a fall. Be ready for anything.

- **Extreme endurance.** You've trained hours every day for years. Despite your screaming hamstrings, know that you have the physical endurance to succeed. Be fit to lead.

- **Mind over matter.** Climbing is seventy-five percent mental. Win the battle of the mind first, and know you will handle stress in the most difficult of situations.

- **Zero defects.** Invest in the tools and clothes required to handle variations in weather and terrain. Cut no corners, and pursue only perfection.

- **Fanatical self-discipline.** From proper planning to mimicking our climbing guide's every move, radical discipline separates the boys from the men.

- **Care of self.** Even if you lose your appetite or feel the pressure to meet a deadline, eat, drink and rest at breaks. I can only take care of others after taking care of myself.

What can stop you from elevation? Nothing except yourself.

Dig deep for the strength within, continue your march across whatever glaciers and steep snowfields you face. Resist the wind and cold of opposition, crest the summit with elation. And don't forget to celebrate.

With each summit you conquer, you'll learn more about yourself and your leadership abilities. Learn to elevate as the slope rises. Make it an unspoken covenant with those you lead.

Climb on!

ELEVATION: RECOGNIZING THE CHALLENGES AHEAD

As the slope rises, leadership must rise. The unwritten covenant of leading people is: To be the leader I aspire to be, I must elevate to match the slope before me. Anyone can lead when the terrain is flat or only moderately inclined, but there comes a time when the journey leads to a peak. It's on this trail where leadership is tested, validated, and honed.

A few months back I spoke on elevation and someone asked, "How do I know I and/or my team need to elevate?" That's a great question.

How do you know you need to elevate? Self-awareness. Take a good look in the mirror.

- **Comfort.** If you feel everything is comfortable, you're probably stagnating. Comfort is cozy but retards growth.

- **Perfection.** When you believe everything is fine, or you've reached the top.

- **Reality.** When you are unable to distinguish the top ten percent of your staff from the pack because they are all "best in class."

- **Self-evaluation.** When you do your annual review, you think you are a perfect performer.

- **Invincibility.** You talk more about past accomplishments than the work ahead.

How do you get your team to realize they need to elevate?

First, admit your own need to elevate, and then make necessary changes. Second, provide clarity concerning expectations and hold others accountable. Finally, share behavioral examples of what it means to elevate. The gaps should be self-evident. Sharing what it means to elevate helps even the most defensive person begin to see a need for change.

Here are a few behavioral examples to begin with. Elevation is:

- **Manic attention to detail.** Mistakes happen and I make them—we all make them. That said, when I make mistakes because of lack of attention, it makes me look sloppy and robs us of hard fought wins. When I'm late, turn in inaccurate numbers, neglect to spellcheck, screw up email, storage, etc., it damages my credibility. If I lose credibility, I lose my ability to lead.

- **Loving my people by disciplining them when warranted.** Just as I lavish praise and recognition for incredible performances, I must balance that with discipline. Praise should be public, but discipline should always be private.

- **Leading my customers.** Customers are not always right. Steve Jobs recognized this. He knew the concepts customers wanted, designed from there and led. Traditional IT simply responds to customers. They are order takers. That worked in the past but will not work in the future as competition rises. I must be unafraid to lead my customers, even when a customer does not want to be led.

- **My team is never my enemy.** We are a team, and we don't have time to waste fighting one another. I address team conflicts within the context of organizational values and keep it inside our own house. Don't go outside of this boundary. Don't complain to the customer. They have their own issues and don't want to hear about ours.

- **Assertiveness.** I tire of hearing lame excuses about why things are delayed, i.e., waiting on so-so to call or email me, or "The reason we have poor performers is because of HR." No, I don't buy that. I pick up the phone or go to their office. Make it happen. The ball is in my court.

- **Messaging commander's intent throughout your organization.** If the captain says take the north hill, we take the north hill. If I allow the message to be reinterpreted, I'll find staff taking the south hill. If there's a major disconnect between what's ordered and what people do, it's a leadership issue.

- **Evaluating employees honestly.** If the majority were top performers, we'd have a perfect organization. We don't. If I'm friendly-to-a-fault with some of my subordinates, this might blind me, so I must constantly seek out external opinions. If a staff member loses their position, am I concerned more about that impact on our mission or the impact on them? My primary concern should always be the organization.

- **Knowing I need to elevate.** Most do not perceive the need for elevation. Leaders elevate constantly. Period.

- **Knowing the mind gives out before the body.** Train myself to be strong in mind and my body will follow. Healthy mind, healthy body.

- **Ownership.** Own problems. Don't play ticket tennis. Never give up. Don't point fingers. Take responsibility and practice accountability.

- **Busting silos.** If someone is bleeding, should I wait for a medic since I'm not the medic? No, I go stop the bleeding. Don't let artificial barriers keep you from action.

- **Continuous self-improvement.** Don't wait for a required book study or a class to come along. Ask: How am I better than last year? How have I transformed myself?

- **Line of sight.** Knowing how my efforts lead to the fulfillment of organizational objectives. I must know my individual staff's mission and my staff should know mine. Collectively our mission should inspire all of us.

- **Going eye to eye.** Directly address those I've been entrusted to serve (lead). Never ever deliver difficult messages via any other means but eye to eye. Never.

- **Sharing myself.** Giving of myself to those I'm entrusted to serve.

Leadership is tough, especially when the slope rises. You may reach a point along the journey where you hit your limit. That's okay. Recognize it and deal with it. Not everyone reaches the summit. Most mountain expeditions have less than a fifty percent success rate. Smart climbers know their limits. They stop and turn around to avoid disaster. Sometimes you need to head back down and regroup before you start back up. If you have reached your limit, it might be best to let someone else lead.

ACTIVE DUTY DENIED! ADJUST AND ADAPT

This was probably one of the hardest things I had to go through in my life. It impacted who I was as a man and my dreams. It is not a story I enjoy telling and, in fact, this is the first time I have shared this story with anyone but my wife.

I am someone who hates rejection—hate it. I had a rough time getting to and through college, but I was getting things together with my life. I had found my faith, Julie and I had recently married and we were laying out our plan going forward. The plan was for me to go on active duty in the Army, become a second lieutenant and have enough money to get established, start our family and build a career. One of my long-term dreams was to be an army officer and eventually rise to the rank of full bird colonel.

As it turned out we ended up getting pregnant a little ahead of plan, and so moving into the active duty Army as an officer was really a critical piece of our life plan. There was a lot riding on it. It was also important from a stability point of view for us. Julie would graduate with me while six months pregnant.

So I began the process of becoming an Army officer as a cadet. At various times, about sixty percent of cadets who wanted to be on active duty would obtain that status. The rest were relegated to Reserve status. There are a lot of different criteria used to select you for an active duty slot. I was starting at a disadvantage since I had a horrible GPA in school—at one point I had a 1.6 GPA. That alone would be difficult to overcome.

In the Army ROTC program you are rated on your performance on a scale from 1 to 5. If you can get consistent 5 ratings you are almost guaranteed an active duty spot. As you head downward in the ratings, your chances grow slimmer and slimmer. Most people get a rating of 3, or average.

I knew that because of my academic background, my main hope to for active duty was to consistently earn fives. The advantage I had over most cadets was that I had previously been in the Army as a combat medic. I had background most did not and it gave me a slight advantage. I knew enough that I could prepare better for what was coming. I also knew that the first week in camp would be about physical fitness, map reading, and other subjects I knew well.

That first week I was pretty much perfect. I was riding high at the top of my class. Things went downhill after that—all of the things I subsequently did were pretty much average and that dragged down my final rating to a three.

Well, now our plans to graduate from college and start our family were in jeopardy because it did not look as though I was going to get an active duty posting. Sure enough, the decision came back and I was not offered an active duty spot.

I was crushed. I was devastated. All of our plans were dependent on me getting a second lieutenant posting. We were pregnant and I was asking myself, *what am I going to do with my life?* There I was with a psychology degree—the only degree I could get with my grades—but what could I do with that? At the least I had to figure out a way to leverage a business or engineering degree.

I was twenty-one years old and this was the toughest challenge I had faced.

On top of knowing we could not go forward as planned, was the personal sense of failure I felt as well as the embarrassment and shame that went along with it. How was I going to tell everyone? How would I face my family and my peers? I was just starting life and already I had failed.

Looking back at it now, perhaps it was not as bad as I thought at the time, but back then it was bad. We had to find a way to overcome and adapt.

I think it was fortunate that this happened to me—I should say, to *us*—at such an early age. It really tested us. We worked through it over the following months and years, and that really helped strengthen not just our relationship, but also our personal resolve.

We went through some very hard times. We had to re-tool our plans and come up with a new path. For the next year and a half we lived very cheaply, taking public assistance while I went to graduate school. I was able to get my master's degree and that opened doors for me.

We persevered. We failed forward. We did not lose hope or our faith, and we came out the better for it on the other end.

FAIL FORWARD

fail (fāl), v.i.
1. to fall short of success or achievement in something expected, attempted, desired or approved: The experiment failed because of poor planning.

You will fail, especially if you take risks. The key is to fail forward. Learn from your mistakes and negative circumstances.

Most of us tend to forget how or why we failed and are doomed to repeat the same mistakes. The more you fail forward, the more adept you become with resiliency. The more you fail forward, the more confidence you gain and the more confidence you have, the higher likelihood of extraordinary tales.

How can I learn from mistakes and share those lessons with others? Failure is critical to success. It's like skiing and never falling. If you want to get better you have to fall. You have to fail.

Fail forward.

THE SECRET TO GREAT SEX...
AND OTHER FAUX PAS ALONG MY JOURNEY

Skipping the rank of manager, I catapulted from physician relations coordinator to director of information technology. I had worked plenty with a cadre of nurse directors at my former employer, so I expected the same stereotype when I landed at Parkview Episcopal Medical Center. Boy was I wrong!

My first week after orientation, I attended a mandatory leadership class on counseling employees using a new behavioral technique. After the theory lesson, we were randomly partnered with a peer to practice our newly acquired skills. My partner was the director of surgical services, and she was a young knockout. I had expected someone seasoned in looks and experience, but this woman made me nervous.

I hate to disappoint any of you readers, but I was struggling. I was afraid that my subconscious might win over my conscious and I would say something bad. I was coaching myself to not say any word that might even remotely sound sexual or land me in trouble. I recall moving into her personal space, per instruction, locking eyes and going through our training script, fumbling for words. I started to sweat but made it through. *Phew!* Deep breath. She then began. She moved in, locked eyes and with all sincerity asked me, "What is your secret to great sex?"

She quickly corrected, "secret to *success*," but it was too late. Our uncontrollable laughter lasted a good 15 minutes. The instructor moved us to the corner of the room because we were disrupting others. It was the hardest I had laughed, ever. We eventually regained composure, and a great working relationship was born. Adding to the drama, the next morning at 7 a.m., I presented to the surgical committee and she was sitting there smiling—obviously thinking the same thing as I was. I had to look away.

Over the years, I created many faux pas or bloopers. Here are some of the best:

- I re-gifted some chocolates only to learn from the recipient that when they opened the box, the original thank you note meant for me was inside.

- I replied to an email from our Chief Medical Information Officer (CMIO) that had been generated inside of our internal collaboration software. He relayed his concern regarding a public posting from another physician that might have violated our solicitation policy. I replied that not only was it a gross violation, but that the doctor had frequently done this on my Facebook page as well. About five minutes later, another colleague sent me a note asking me if I knew that my reply was posted to every employee instead of just my CMIO.

- I was speaking with two fellow officers when a third one joined our conversation. I said with utmost sincerity, "Hey, here is our best hospital president in the entire health system." As soon as I let that loose, I realized the other two were also hospital presidents.

- Our COO was wrapping up his closing remarks after an all-day leadership meeting. The technical aspects went without a glitch. I instant messaged the admin who was "running" the operation when, lo and behold, my IM popped up on screen, on top of the presentation. *"Phew, so glad the technology worked for once."* I shrank in my chair as the audience chuckled.

- I was dancing the night away at an after work party. While I prefer ballroom and Argentine Tango, I can hold my own in freestyle, or so I thought. The people who could clearly "move like Jagger" later told me that I "danced like a white man." I don't know if that's an offensive statement to anyone else, but to me it said that I danced like a dork, or at least that's how it made me feel.

- One of my nurse managers had been asking to go out to lunch, and I was forced to cancel twice. Finally, my schedule opened up, so I teasingly messaged her "Our time has finally come to be together." She agreed to meet me in our lobby at the appointed hour. I was shocked when a different nurse manager showed up and realized I had asked the wrong person out. Talk about an awkward lunch!

- Sexting to the wrong person. I have not done this yet but know it's only a matter of time. My wife and I exchange all sorts of texts from "pick up some eggs on the way home" to…well use your imagination! Someday I am certain it will go the wrong person. Hopefully not my HR colleagues!

Over the years, I've learned to laugh at myself. My foibles and blunders will be around as long as I'm alive. It's called being human, and we can't take ourselves too seriously. Ever. Do you commit a workplace faux pas that you can only respond to with laughter?

BIGGEST BLUNDERS

Experience is not always the best teacher. Learning from other people's experiences is better. Another person's evaluated experience trumps them all. Unfortunately, I am prone to learning things the hard way. To keep this book short, I have focused only on my professional blunders. My personal mistakes would take up too far much space.

People

Hiring too quickly. In an effort to fill a role expediently, I once compromised standards. I failed to vet candidates adequately. The person I hired caused pain for everyone. One day I spent more time counseling and repairing damage to a particular senior staff person than I did on business. As one known for having the most competent senior team, my credibility took two steps back. As a result, I'm more deliberate today in making sure each fit is solid, even if that means leaving a position unfilled.

Firing too slowly. Way too slowly. I have allowed people to stay, causing more harm than good. I've also let others dictate who I keep. When I finally mustered the courage to do the firing, the person fired was more relieved than I was. I learned that the energy required to salvage the wrong person is better put to use developing top performers.

Process

Always consider your audience before acting. Emphasizing the need for physical security, I had our security analysts make a habit of gathering unsecured, unattended devices. An analyst left behind a card instructing the owner of one such device to retrieve it from my office. Analysts had a green light to confiscate unsecured executive laptops as well. When the CEO came to my office to retrieve his device, it was a bit of an awkward moment. I learned to think about all the possible outcomes of my directives, and make adjustments while still enforcing protocol.

Do personal business at home. I spent a weekend in Colorado presiding over a management meeting for a successful rock band. We spent time knocking out an internal contract about royalties and responsibilities as well as rules of the road. In an effort to disseminate quickly, I sent the documents from my work email. I inadvertently sent it to my IT department. Embarrassed, I learned not to send personal documents from work.

Dress the part. I did not pick up on the fashion hints offered by my CEO. Finally, the CFO pulled me aside and said, "Ed, compared to your predecessor, you have two shortcomings. One is experience (I was 35), which we knew when we promoted you, and that's not a concern. But the second is…you don't dress the part." He handed me a business card for the clothier the exec staff used. Message received, and I revamped my wardrobe. Your clothes and style do speak volumes.

The wrong position. "But it's the dream job, the one I've been waiting for." I downplayed the red flags. I recall vendor executives as well as former employees giving me fair warning, but I dismissed them. As I soon found out they were right, I dealt with the consequences. I made the best of a compromised situation, but in hindsight, I should have listened to wise counsel and proceeded differently.

Leadership

Walking in authority. I had been promoted internally to CIO, but other employees (including myself) still saw me as the Deputy CIO. This attitude diminished the strategic nature of our division, and I allowed one executive in particular to mistreat my team. Not until a couple of years later did I begin to walk in my authority and confront such situations. I stood up to the schoolyard bullies, and then things changed.

Pay me now or pay me *more* later. Capital investments are limited, and every division wants some. I did the political thing and deferred to others, which put our technology infrastructure at risk. If I had fought harder to ensure funding, we would not have faced a crisis that later arose from this error. Given the impact of IT in clinical and business operations, I have vowed not to fail in this respect again.

This is not an exhaustive list but contains the mistakes that most haunt me. What about you? What mistakes have you made that would benefit those around you so they don't have to learn the *hard way*?

GETTING FIRED FROM MY FIRST REAL JOB

My first professional job was working for Teledyne Waterpik. When I was going to school I knew that I really wanted to work in healthcare. But it was really hard to find a job so I was looking at anything I could get. Teledyne was *sort of healthcare related*, so I got myself hired and was told to support the sales team. I actually did some cool things there. I had a great relationship with the sales team but I was really bored.

I had to sit for eight hours while only working two. I had a lot of time to develop new things. I would always go to my boss, the vice president of sales, and ask "what else can I do?" She asked what I wanted to do. I told her about my degree and interest in consumer science. She talked to some of the other vice presidents but nothing ever came of it, so I just kept on working.

On day 89 of my 90 day probationary period I was called in to her office and she was there with the vice president of HR and I was shocked. They were firing me! It was so humbling. It was so hard to come home and tell my wife that I had lost my job.

It was humbling, but also very motivating. I walked in forgiveness and didn't hold a grudge against my former boss. It made me stronger and pushed me through some tough times until I finally got the job in healthcare that I wanted. Years later after being very successful in several jobs, I ran into my former boss at the hospital one day. She recognized me and saw my badge. I told her that I was really happy and glad that things had gone the way they had and worked out the way they did.

ALMOST GETTING BOOTED FROM BOOT CAMP

When I joined the Army I almost got kicked out of basic training because of my lack of fitness.

When that happened, I told myself that this would never happen again. It was so embarrassing! They have this test, the APFT (Army Physical Fitness Test) and it has a maximum score of 300 points. You have to get 60 points to pass it. It's made up of lots of fitness tests: pushups, pull-ups, running, etc. I flunked the first time I took it and vowed then and there to only get perfect 300 point scores from then going forward. Getting a perfect score is very difficult—only a few people get them each year. So I started working on my pushup and pull-ups and I got to the point where I was getting 290s and above, which put me in a very elite category of the military.

In the late 1980s, Congresswoman Patricia Schroeder of Colorado wanted the most physically fit member of the military in Colorado to go out and run with President Clinton the next time he was in Colorado. Based on the APFT scores, I was judged the most fit military person in Colorado and it was amazing considering where I had come from.

I never actually got to run with the President, but I took great pride in the way I brought myself back from the brink of failure.

9
WONDERMENT AND CONTINUOUS LEARNING

lear • ning (lûr′ning), n.
1. knowledge acquired by systematic study in any field of scholarly application. 2. the act or process of acquiring knowledge or skill.

I love the term *wonderment*. It's such a descriptive word. I am always trying to learn something new and try something different and I love the sense of wonder I feel when I experience something for the first time. It's a rush and it's invigorating.

When I got into IT—healthcare IT in particular—I could not understand why we as a profession would not be the most technologically advanced group in the work place. I was stunned to find brilliant people trapped under the technological constraints of what they had learned ten or twenty years before. No thinking outside the box.

I always want to learn more. I always want to find something new to be passionate about and I have found that I am passionate about learning because learning is *always* about something new. I switch out and get new tech (devices) each year. I am constantly reading everything—inside and out of my industry. I am always studying.

Most of us graduate and think of learning as a closed chapter in our lives. The number of adults who have not read a book or embraced additional learning opportunities (unforced) is numbing.

The more inputs you can create in your life, from work to hobbies, from the arts to sports, the more opportunities you have to accomplish amazing things. The exposure and input you receive from experiencing different personalities to skills to ideas is essential for extraordinary tales to become commonplace.

How Snow White Changed my Life

Okay, *life change* is a stretch, but Snow White and some of her princess peers do remind me of a critical aspect of leadership—the creation of special moments. Disney promises to be "where dreams come true." For Starbucks aficionados, myself included, it's the belief that "handcrafted beverages are the secret to making life better." Five years ago, I added "create perfect moments" to my personal strategic plan. It's a reminder to myself to ensure "creating perfect moments" moves from bench to bedside. In the workplace, this strategy has worked well. In my personal life? Well, let me tell you about that.

While in Orlando recently, I spent time exploring Disney's Epcot. Just for fun, and to make my wife and 20-year-old daughter smile, I decided to grab a photo op with Snow White. Was my pride ever challenged! There I was, sandwiched between animated toddlers and star struck preteens, in line to take a picture with Ms. Purity herself. Seemed everyone was dressed like a princess except me. I stood close to one toddler hoping passersby would think I was part of her family. Heaven forbid someone I knew might see me standing in line at Disney for a personal princess pic!

My turn came, and I sheepishly held my arm out for Snow White. My friend took the picture. I was ready to run, but Snow would not let me go. *Help!* She turned, looked me in the eye, and engaged me in conversation. I was pulling away but she kept me there. It was longer than a moment but not excessive, maintaining eye contact the entire time. As if someone just discovered my hand in the cookie jar, I was about to break out in a nervous sweat.

I texted the picture to my wife and daughter, and they both replied ROT-FL. So when I saw Sleeping Beauty, I stepped in line again. This time I carefully observed all the interactions between the princess and her devotees. Ms. Beauty held eye contact with every fan and, though brief, engaged in conversation. My turn came and, though I tried to pull away, she clung to my arm until we talked. Awkward, yes, but so enlightening. Ditto with Belle, Cinderella, and last but not least, Ariel. They were indeed making dreams come true for their fans. They made me feel important.

So how can we take something as simple and yet profound as a Disney princess engagement formula and put it into practice for ourselves? How can we allow the creation of special moments to become a natural part of who we are?

As leaders, we are so rushed. I'm preaching to myself here. We walk past our staff with nary an acknowledgement. When we do stop to talk, we are thinking about the meeting we are headed to. On one hand, we claim that the right people in the right places are our most valuable assets. But do we give them the gift of our time, fully present, even for just a minute? This points to a contradiction in basic leadership style.

Since my return from Disney, I've been doubling down in the creating of special moments, with a focus on my staff. I am making sure every interaction, however brief, is meaningful. Eye contact. Genuine interest. While the other person may be rushed, I will remind myself that my agenda is their agenda, and my role as a leader is to serve them. True, not every person will want the time, but for those who do, I am there.

Before the end of my last day at Epcot, I was looking for another princess. Why? Because I enjoyed the way they made me feel. Special. If a play actor princess can do this much for strangers, we can do it for those we serve. Pics or no pics.

Create special moments.

EXPERIENCE IS NOT THE BEST TEACHER

We took our youngest child Talitha on her first visit to Kauai so she could visit her grandparents. This is the same couple who, years earlier, offered me a bribe not to marry their daughter. They had retired to a condo, high overlooking the Na Pali coast. One day while they babysat Talitha, my wife Julie and I headed out for adventure with our eight-year-old son Brandon and a German exchange student, Sonja. We began our day intent on making it to Secret Falls, only accessible by foot.

We rented two kayaks, donned lifejackets, and started paddling up the Wailua River to the remote trailhead two klicks away. The evening before, a major storm passed through, so our outfitters warned us that the river would be more challenging than normal to navigate.

Julie and Sonja paddled smoothly and held a great line down the middle of the river. Brandon and I had a difficult time keeping the keel pointed upstream as we beached the banks. A mile in, we came to a choke point where the placid river channeled into a quarter of its normal width, creating a high velocity flow with rapids and eddies. The women stopped short of the rushing waters and, of course, we men decided to show them how to row into the strait, like salmon looking to spawn. Half way in, I realized we had no chance. I tried to turn the kayak 180° to go back in search of an alternate route.

The kayak flipped. I fell out, and the current sucked me ten yards downstream into a recessed pool. The upside-down kayak remained in the turbulent waters, tangled in branches and storm debris. The women witnessed this and moved in as close as they could while staying in waters that were manageable. No one could see Brandon, and we were afraid he'd been swept under and caught in debris. A muffled "Help!" reached our ears. He could not escape because his life jacket's buoyancy was keeping him trapped in an air pocket under the kayak.

Julie's mother-bear instincts kicked in. She jumped into the water and swam to the kayak. Grabbing smooth but slippery tree roots along the bank, I pulled myself to the other end of the vessel. Between the two of us, we were able to flip the craft. Brandon floated into the calm pool to safety. We decided the best course of action would be to carry our kayaks on land past the channel and then get back in.

While we collected ourselves, a man and his son rowed past us. They had observed the scene and congratulated us on our remarkable recovery. They then proceeded past us thinking they could muscle their way through the current. Sure enough, at the midpoint, the father turned the kayak to head back. As if in a bad rerun, they also flipped, and the kayak got stuck in the same spot. The dad stayed upstream, holding onto branches. His son was nowhere in sight. No muffled cries for help. He had seat belted himself in. So not only was he under the kayak, but upside down submerged. I jumped back in and made way to the kayak. We could not flip it given the physics with his son as anchor. Reaching under, I pulled at every strap I could find to break the boy free. Likely seconds but seemingly minutes, he was freed. We eventually got him to shore, shaken but alive.

Julie and I talked afterwards and wondered why on earth our fellow paddlers made the decision to copy our near tragedy. After observing our experience, why would they even *want* to follow our path? Sure, had we been successful it would have made sense. But we nearly lost our son.

First-hand experience is not always the best teacher. Had this father taken note of our experience, he could have spared his son the anxiety and fear that comes from nearly drowning.

So it is in work. Why do we insist on replicating another leader's or organization's failures? Why don't we take advantage of their experience, both the good and the bad? Is it pride? Is it a feeling of invincibility? Arrogance? Fear?

The next time you embark on a journey, prepare in advance. Use two parts planning to one part execution. Research leading practices. Study accounts of success and failures related to your endeavor. I learned this from one of my mentors. Before embarking on our Electronic Health Records journey, he insisted we contact successful and unsuccessful organizations and learn. I arranged several CEO/CIO meetings with peer health systems where we actively learned from others' experiences. It paid off and is now part of my standard way of operating.

Learn from other's mistakes; benefit from their experience.

WHEN THE WORST IS BEST.

Years ago, I played on a church softball team. We lost every game we played in our city league for multiple seasons. Some team members were proud of the fact we were well known for our "good attitudes and behavior," but I wanted no part of a losing team, bad or good attitudes aside. I figured if we won a few games along the way, our good-sportsmanship reputation would be better respected. I stayed engaged and, as the best player on the team, was eventually asked to manage the team. I essentially took over these "Bad News Bears."

Early the next spring, I held tryouts. I also secured a sponsor who provided us with all the equipment and uniforms necessary to field a team. My criteria for selecting players? In addition to good attitudes, they had to be better players than me. I could hold my own fielding and batting so I figured if I were the threshold, we would be competitive.

We practiced. We scouted our opposition. We started winning. In making lineup adjustments, I eventually scratched myself out of the starting lineup. We took first place in our league and won tournaments. We were now known for good sportsmanship and as the team to beat. Fun and satisfying! I still have all the trophies boxed up in the attic, unable to let them go. What I learned about leadership and teamwork during my softball days helped shape who I am today.

My objectives at work are similar. As I build teams, my goal is to be the least talented and gifted leader. If I represent the threshold, I have confidence we will serve our organization well. You have heard the adage that "C" leaders hire "D" players, "B" leaders hire "C" players, but *"A" leaders hire "A+" players.* My ultimate objective is to eventually work myself out of a job. When a leader leaves an organization, that organization shouldn't skip a beat and ideally should move forward even faster under new leadership.

Hiring and cultivating leaders who are—or can become—better than you takes confidence. It's an intimidating step that will expose insecurities you didn't know you had. Fight through your weaknesses and any self-doubts. Learn from your team. But be careful! Don't let your insecurities interfere. Don't sabotage the leaders on your team out of your own fear. Put on your big boy pants and die to yourself.

Die. To. Your. Self.

Here's the deal. Being the best on your team limits your organization's potential. Being the best in a position where you've reached the top means you can't learn from those around you. Where is the genuine satisfaction in that?

If I insisted on being the best player on my softball team, I would've made great plays and batted in some runs, but would we have won? Probably not. Sure, I would've received plenty of ego strokes, but at what price?

Ironically, not only did our softball team win, but I improved as a player. At work, I continually grow. Why? Because my team continues to grow. Funny how that works.

GET OFF OF MY CLOUD!

1960s entertainment anticipated the future. Star Trek tricorders are here. Lapel communicators are ubiquitous. And who can forget the Rolling Stones singing about their "Cloud?"

Most agree mobility and agility are the future. The cloud is infrastructure that enables both mobility and agility. The cloud is the reinvention of computing as a service, not a product, akin to a utility. The cloud enables technology to accelerate the speed of business.

Friends recently returned from a trip abroad. The advanced wireless infrastructures found in Third World countries both astounded and pleased them. By unintentionally leapfrogging the technological revolution, these regions had bypassed the incremental advancements of the last thirty years and gone straight from laggards to leaders. Societies that never had a telephony infrastructure, suddenly are experiencing the highest per capita numbers of cellular subscribers.

Advancement by leapfrogging. Can we do this in healthcare IT? Maybe a better question to ask is, *do we need to?*

YES! Mobility, enabled by the cloud, is the path to the future.

Healthcare organizations viewed as laggards now have the potential to leapfrog peers. The cloud will empower us, enabling the bypassing of heavy capital investment, letting us eliminate kludgy hardware while rendering single organization data centers obsolete. New data strategies can shrink implementation timelines from months to weeks. Focus your institution on implementation and optimization rather than worrying over floor space or cooling requirements.

If we don't transform our organizations by routing capital away from brick and mortar to cloud-based mobile applications and services, the Third World will pass us up.

As legacy hardware and software contracts expire, look for cloud alternatives. Basic requirements for any new application should include cloud capabilities. If the vendor has no cloud offering, be concerned. Ask deep questions. You don't want your calendar to announce 2015 with you still struggling with data centers bursting at the seams with legacy applications residing on heavy iron.

The cloud has been around for several years in one form or another. Non-healthcare industries have embraced the cloud successfully. Some worry about security, yet the number of incidents are no different in the cloud versus in-house. Breaches occur in both. Security is not the barrier.

As a leader, show courage. Move your organization forward. Become relevant by leveraging mobility. Lead by learning! Embrace the cloud!

Hey you, *get onto my cloud!*

Caught, not Taught

As a parent, the most frightening rite of passage for me to tackle was not "the sex talk." It was "the car talk." As in, watching my kids drive down the street solo in a two-thousand pound, steel and fiberglass projectile. They had attended classes, studied a manual, and passed a test. But were they really prepared?

Not fully. They lacked one critical element.

In the workplace, I advocate professional development and have witnessed the benefits of classroom teaching. When I began to analyze this process, however, I realized traditional training was limited to a maximum effectiveness. Think about this. After reading a book on teamwork, were you able to convert all the learned lessons into action? Why do some managers respond to training while their classmates do not? Why do some leaders take life-changing courses, yet nothing changes?

Critical skills can only be caught, not taught. My children, for example, had the head knowledge for driving, but that information didn't come alive for them until they took it on the road. Experiencing the streets helped them to *catch*—or ingrain—the skills for successful driving.

How do you help your team catch? Ability to drive is a necessity that comes with an inherent motivator—drive or be stuck living under my roof with my rules!

So how can you create a learning-to-drive context that will motivate your staff to live out what they learned from books? The following methods have worked for me.

Never Fly Solo. Do your best to always have a sidekick with you. If I have a team member in the hospital or a funeral to attend, I take an emerging leader with me to help provide comfort. When I walk around to visit the team, I have a manager with me so they can learn from the experience through observation and active participation.

Be Vulnerable. When I have tough decisions to make or challenges to contend with, I open the kimono. I don't "shelter" my team or pretend to know the answers. I include them. The young leader learns there is no voodoo or secret sauce. Some day they will face a similar issue and it will be familiar.

Share the Stage. When I'm invited to speak, write, or interview, I often have one of my leaders with me. Sometimes observing and other times co-presenting. One of our young directors had not presented before. I had him observe me at a local university. The next time we co-presented. Now he speaks routinely on the national stage.

Be Transparent. Leverage social and business media. On Facebook, I add as "friends" any of my team who has interest in being connected. I connect with any of them on Twitter or LinkedIn. In the work environment, I microblog daily about what I am doing and why. This allows multiple avenues for insight. For instance, I may share my thought process on how I deal with setbacks.

Engage a Mentor. Ongoing, planned partnerships focus on helping a person reach specific goals over a pre-determined period. Unfortunately, the art of mentoring is still catching on in the business world, healthcare included. Mentoring can be a difference maker.

Connect to Others. As a leader, how do I impact the heart of my team? How do I create an environment where we can cultivate compassion? How do I help them view their job as more than a paycheck, but as a contribution to a patient's life?

Ask Questions. Whenever I'm around people I admire, I fire off a number of questions then just listen and learn. I soak up wisdom.

Create Hang Time. It's easier to talk when we're not disguised in stuffy work attire. A non-business setting encourages conversation. But you have to create these situations. I have surprised my team with ice cream socials. I invite individual team members to attend employer-sponsored professional sports events with me. I attend their amateur symphony performances or listen to their garage bands at a local bar. I invite them to join my family for Broadway shows (we always buy extra tickets). Make it happen!

Offer Social Opportunities. Do you learn etiquette from a manual? Emerging leaders who seek to become vice presidents should know how to handle themselves in a "cocktail party" situation and know things like the difference between red and white wines. My wife and I purposely host parties in our home to create a safe place in which they can practice and learn to be comfortable mingling with other executives. .

Outcomes?

I've had the joy of watching my direct reports blossom in their careers. Although I invested greatly in their formal training, their development accelerates during active observation. In the last couple of years, several became CIOs. Others took senior leadership positions in professional organizations.

My kids did turn out to be pretty good drivers. But if you ask them how they learned, they'll tell you they *caught* it by doing it—by making wrong turns, slamming on the brakes at stoplights, bumping over curbs while parallel parking. The driver's manual finally made sense to them.

Caught, not taught.

TRANSFORMATION THROUGH THE WRITTEN WORD

My nephew, Jordan, while still in high school, was thinking about careers. Spring Break of 2009 found him shadowing his "Uncle Ed" to explore the world of healthcare. He met with me each morning for 5 a.m. workouts and shadowed me until we returned home for 6 p.m. family dinners. Free time was spent developing content for an innovation workshop he would help me lead for one of our hospital leadership teams.

We nailed the workshop. The hospital president was so impressed with Jordan's facilitation techniques that he offered him a job upon college graduation. We left that Friday session exhausted but high, ready for a Starbucks reward! Immersed all week in healthcare and spending time with physicians and leaders, his career decision crystallized. After graduating as class valedictorian, Jordan began an eight-year journey as a University of Colorado Medical School BA/BS-MD student, one of only ten so chosen in the nation.

An elite runner, Jordan serves me humble pie each time we connect and put in a few hard miles. A college freshman, he asked me for my views on Atul Gawandi's *The Checklist Manifesto* and how it had influenced our culture. A month later he asked me about Franz Johansson's *The Medici Effect: What Elephants and Epidemics Can Teach Us About Innovation*. We met up recently in Denver, and, during this run, he wanted to know my views on George Johnson's *Fire in the Mind: Science, Faith, and the Search for Order.* "Uncle Ed, where does science end and religion begin?" He loses me on the hill. Is this my nineteen-year-old nephew?

The more I learn about his medical school program and curriculum, the more impressed I am. They have something special happening at the University of Colorado School of Medicine with their focus on stimulating personal and professional growth through book studies. Every other week, these future physicians tackle another book and vigorously debate its meaning.

Book and debate reinforced my IT department's approach. I was not a reader in my youth, but as my hunger grew for leadership, I began devouring the written page. A causal correlation emerged. The more I learned, the more effective I became. I asked my direct reports to read with me, and I observed the same causality. If these book studies were helpful for my teams, then what about my entire organization?

Twelve years and counting, still my desire for continuous learning has not abated. I have seen the transformative impact it has had on my organizations. Hearing about Jordan's medical school inspired me to continue pressing forward.

Many people stop learning the day they graduate. Countering this with book studies in the work place carries numerous benefits. Studies remove excuses and make learning convenient. The studies bring a cross-section of individuals together who might not otherwise meet each other. Cohorts ensure accountability, and nobody shows up to class unprepared. Relationships form. Engagement deepens. Leadership is honed. New ideas stimulate innovation. Sometimes we invite our strategic partners. Learning happens. People grow.

How to develop a program in your workplace:

- Charge a modest fee for the class. Return the fee for eighty percent attendance. Donate unreturned fees to United Way.

- Lead the first set of classes yourself so you can model the process. Then delegate teaching to your direct reports. Redelegate this to line staff as you find alignment between a participants' passion, ability to teach, and applicability to their needs.

- Classes early in the day have the most traction.

- Books with associated workbooks work especially well.

- Meet weekly and run each class six to eight sessions for one hour.

- Offer a variety of classes quarterly.

Our next family reunion is in Seattle during the summer. If I want to keep up with Jordan, I'd better keep reading!

Why I Fired and Then Rehired Myself

When I was a member of the Cleveland Triathlon Club, we had a New Year's Day tradition of leaping into the icy waters of Lake Erie, wearing nothing but swim trunks to symbolically wash away the old and welcome the new in our lives.

A few years back, I used this event as the demarcation point for firing and rehiring myself. I intend to do this each year going forward. I think we all should give ourselves the pink slip.

Some time back Intel was losing market share and profitability. Consequently, the company floundered. Knowing it was a matter of time before the board would take corrective action, the leadership, Andrew Grove and Gordon Moore, discussed a particular phenomenon they had observed. Nearly every time a company or division installed new leadership or brought in consultants, their outcomes improved. Their conclusion: the new leader came in energized and with a fresh pair of eyes. Knowing he was being evaluated, he took his responsibility more seriously than the former, uninspired leader.

Subsequently, Intel's old leadership had a brainstorm. Why not fire themselves and come back to the job as the "new" leaders? "If existing management want to keep their jobs when the basics of the business are undergoing profound change, they must adopt an outsider's intellectual objectivity." They fired themselves over a weekend, and, after shifting markets (memory chips to microprocessors), Intel became the clear leader in a very competitive market.

At that time, I worked for University Hospitals in Cleveland. Although neither the hospital or IT was in as dire circumstances as Intel had been, we needed to guard against complacency. I challenged my leaders to follow my example and take time over the holidays to reflect.

Pondering how you would approach your position as a new employee is a healthy and worthy assignment. Look at yourself as a potential candidate for your position and then ask: How will I evaluate the talent, change processes, and balance the service mix? Should I alter my interactions with customers, my personal engagement, or my attitude? Will I embrace ideas I formerly rejected/feared? What strategies and tactics will I deploy to ensure business and clinical convergence with the health system? Do I have the fortitude to remove employees that add no value? Am I stretching the boundaries of innovation? Do I demonstrate courage despite resistance? How will I be a better servant...? The variations are endless.

To *survive*, you probably won't need to change anything you're doing. But to *thrive* means constantly reinventing yourself and operating differently. We, as a team, embraced change, adopted an innovation-oriented culture, and began to walk in the fullness of our authority. The title of Dr. Marshall Goldsmith's excellent book, *What Got You Here Won't Get You There,* says it all.

Several other University Hospitals leaders fired and rehired themselves that New Year's Day in 2007. The result? We experienced a dramatic shift moving from transactional to transformational services that had a net impact on our business and clinical operations. Our business, quality, and service metrics shot up to new heights. I experienced exponential growth, both personally and professionally.

Since I no longer live by the Great Lakes, I had to find a new ritual of annual rebirth. One year I decided that hang gliding over the Swiss Alps was a good replacement. As I leapt off the mountain into the alpine chill, I fired myself as CIO. In my own internal shakeup, I let the prior perceptions of my role plummet to the icy depths. By the dawn of the New Year, I had found innovative eyes to view the future. Only *then* did I rehire myself.

Are you willing to give yourself the pink slip?

WELCOME, WELKOMMEN, BIENVENU, BEM-VINDO, BIENVENIDO, VÍTANÝ

My family has a long history of hosting foreign exchange students in our home. Our "extended" family has expanded over the years, and these former students are now doctors, teachers, and actors. We keep in touch with several of the girls and have even visited a couple here and abroad. The experience of a single exchange—a student new to this country, their family back home, the culture they come from—has enriched our world.

I serve on the global healthcare CIO council for a Fortune 50 company.

Each year a dozen of us gather from around the world to help drive corporate strategy. We get a glimpse into the future and where the industry is headed as it relates to technologies on the horizon. We share challenges and solutions. We commiserate. We learn. We advance the corporation, our employers, and ourselves. It is *enriching.*

At one such conference, I sat with CIOs from Brazil, Japan, USA, Singapore, Greece, United Arab Emirates, Taiwan, Bulgaria, Mexico, Canada, Australia and England. (How fitting that the International Olympic Committee shared the conference facility with us in Chicago.) Although we contributed and advanced the mission of the council, the biggest benefit came from the transparent sharing amongst CIOs.

I'm not able to share council-specific outcomes or where my organization is headed strategically, but I can offer these key takeaways:

- Innovative ideas to remove culture as obstacles to transformation
- Creative organization hierarchies that enable velocity
- Leading from the center
- Progressive management of vendors
- The world *is* flat and we have more in common than you think
- Negotiating the C-Suite more effectively
- Leveraging specific technologies to enhance mobility
- Expanded vision

I gained more from this intimate exchange than I could have from a week at a mega-conference or by reading a year's worth of subscriptions. I established relationships with eleven peers who I can now call on as needed. We established bonds through our time together and found that we had common burdens and shared passions. Their diverse backgrounds opened my eyes to fresh thoughts and strategies. Some of us have already exchanged additional ideas and materials to further our organization's success.

The council sponsor benefited and they will develop enhanced products and services to meet our future needs. Our employers will benefit from their investment of our time as we bring back executable ideas for both strategic and operational advancements. And I, like my peers, have personally benefited through this mutual exchange of ideas, cultures, and personalities. It may sound self-aggrandizing, but I believe the world is a better place now.

Seek opportunities on different levels to share in global exchanges, not just professionally, but in your personal life as well. We did this with our foreign exchange students and our life is better because of it.

WHY DICTATORS BURN BOOKS

Sagging IT performance and rising costs symptomized our health system's deterioration. The then-new CEO appointed me interim CIO with the following charge: "Immediately improve IT performance at a lower cost."

Success meant the job was mine. Failure would mean a squandered opportunity.

Although I had several ideas to jumpstart our IT performance in concert with the health system at large, my biggest obstacle would be the nature of our outsourced IT operations. Two years prior, we had completely outsourced WHAT? to three companies who had formed an "unholy" alliance of sorts. All parties had competing agendas. I had to get everyone on the same page, fast.

We narrowed the outsourced parties down to two, then eventually to one manageable vendor. Deploying numerous strategies and tactics, we lowered costs and improved services. During this process, we identified and addressed the single biggest, critical factor: winning the hearts and minds of our staff. The outsourced vendor held allegiance to their stakeholders; the line staff was torn between their new corporate parent and the healthcare organizations under its umbrella. We had to align allegiances and ensure everyone was of one mind and one vision regarding the health system and its patients. This proved to be key to our success.

We achieved a modicum of success working with the vendor leadership, but it wasn't happening fast enough. So we started spending a few minutes of each staff meeting reviewing chapters of relevant books with the intent of getting everyone focused on doing the right things. For many, this was the first time they'd opened a book since graduate school. Some were transformed by what they learned.

Why did dictators burn books, we wondered?

Time pressures for our turnaround continued to build. We were improving services and reducing costs but had very little margin for experimental failures. We needed to do more. What if we provided books to all the staff and kindled a great awakening? Since we were already reaping moderate results from our leaders why not target all of IT? While applying pressure from the top down, couldn't we also encourage radical change from the bottom up, even create a revolution? I was confident that somewhere in the middle we would win hearts and minds and become one of the best leveraged IT organizations in present-day healthcare.

It worked. Fast. We offered four classes per quarter, and each filled within days of being posted. We taught leadership, teamwork, customer service, change management, finance, and more leadership. Staff copied portions of their books, brought them to their managers and directors, and started asking questions, making suggestions. Some started covert studies of their own with teammates. They started changing their approach to work.

The revolution had begun, and nothing could stop it. We continued lowering IT costs while improving services. Our overall health system performance exceeded expectations. We were winning the local market. Wall Street took notice of our financial recovery and prosperity. But most important, our clinical outcomes ranked among the best in the nation.

Our book studies didn't end there. In fact, my greatest joy came during our sixth cycle when, for the first time, all four classes were taught by line staff. No supervisors, managers, directors, or VPs. During my four years as CIO, I witnessed the completion of more than thirty distinct book studies and trained more than 400 staff. We lowered apples to apples costs for IT by over twenty-five percent and quadrupled our externally validated customer satisfaction scores. Revolution at its zenith!

When I became CIO at my next health system, one of my first strategies was to deploy "book studies." I started with my direct reports, and then we added four classes, four quarters per year. I taught the majority of classes the first year so I could meet as many staff members as possible and share my philosophies and passions with them directly. After one year, we had a complete quarter's-worth of classes taught by non-leadership. I continue to teach or attend at least one class per quarter to maintain my professional development.

Now you know why dictators burn books. They fear the power that comes through knowledge and enlightenment. Their answer to that fear is to suppress learning because learning and knowledge are revolutionary. They are afraid of how the written word can cause change, and, if done well, bring revolution.

Lead your own revolution. Embrace the power of books and use them to empower others.

10

WORK YOUR ASS OFF

work (wûrk), n., adj. v.
1. exertion or effort directed to produce or accomplish something; labor, toil.

Average people outperform above-average people with elbow grease. Working your ass off not only shrinks any gap, but frankly enables the average to overtake their more well-heeled competitors in life, work and play.

"There's no glory in practice, but there's no glory without practice."

Few people truly know what it really takes to succeed—you have to work your ass off. Nobody is born to achieve at high levels, you must work hard to stay competitive while continuing to improve. You need to have a life-long resolve to work your ass off.

It's the same in relationships. Marriage is hard. You have to work hard to be a good dad or brother or sister or mom. Things will happen when you do that. The commitment is far more than working 9-5 and just showing up. There's hardly any traffic on the extra mile.

It's not only important to work your ass off, but you must also balance that work with by celebrating your victories and taking time to rest.

No Pain, No Gain

Sounds trite, I know. Some will accuse me of simplemindedness. Others will say this high school football coach philosophy is dangerous. I agree, but still embrace this concept.

In my thirties, I got back into playing tennis and started thrashing on the courts with some friends from work. As we verged on competitive levels, I realized we needed to pick up our intensity. A consistent first serve was the performance key. Reliance on the second serve would allow your opponent to take the offensive. Although a high first-serve percentage alone would not make you a Wimbledon champion, you could at least guarantee yourself a quarter final match. We practiced at 6 a.m. three times a week, but I always showed up at 5 a.m. to serve buckets and buckets of balls. Then I'd chase them down and start over again.

NO PAIN, NO GAIN.

In my forties, I took on the challenge of perfecting the Argentine Tango with my wife Julie. In addition to a weekly two-hour lesson and a monthly *milonga* (an event where we gather to dance), we practiced. Even if it was for only twenty minutes, we practiced every evening. We had to, because the Argentine Tango happens to be the most artistic, intellectual, and difficult dance ever created by man. If I catch my partner's foot too late, we miss our sweep. If we're too far apart, one of us loses their balance. I figure if we aim for expert, we might reach basic proficiency by the time I'm eighty.

Like our dancing, my relationship with my bride of twenty-nine years has been full of ups and downs. The overall trend slopes upwards to the right, but it's interrupted by numerous peaks and valleys. Some downturns take years to correct, yet we keep at it through annual strategic planning vacations, countless marriage conferences, lots of books, prayer and counsel. We have fought hard to reach the point we're at today, and there is more pain to endure, I'm sure. Had we not chosen to push through the pain of the valleys, who knows where our marriage would be? Certainly not growing and not moving forward.

And what about your career? Can you ascend the leadership ranks by good luck or good looks? Not in my case. It took pain—blood, sweat, and tears. No shortcuts. No submitting "C"-level work. No shaving time here and there to start the weekend early.

But it's so tempting!

I hear you. But do you want to reach the fulfillment of your calling? Then sacrifice. Embrace pain.

A few years back, I had to spend a significant amount of time on the road. The librarian at Parkview Episcopal Medical Center in Colorado where I was working at the time supplied me with endless materials, from business books on tape to vocabulary building materials. While driving, I'd listen to these resources over and over until they became part of my intellectual fabric. Would have I preferred to listen to U2 or another favorite band? Of course. But to grow, I needed to take advantage of every morsel of time.

I also volunteered for everything in my path; some related to IT, others benefited the hospital or another department. Would I have preferred to go home early or have a smaller to-do list? Certainly. But to maximize my potential and opportunity, I needed to self-sacrifice—so far as it didn't harm my family. Plus, it was only for a season. Every season brings different opportunities, each of which require fitting sacrifices.

Today, I've made sure we have a library of materials available for our staff to check out—hundreds of CDs and books on tape. We have subscriptions for "book of the month," a concept I leveraged from the Parkview librarian. Just as serving thousands of tennis balls to ghosts at the break of dawn paved the way to winning several tournaments; or investing the time and money to improving my tango kept me on the dance floor, pain brings gain.

Don't expect to just show up on the dance floor and look like a pro. If you want someone to ask you to dance, practice.

No pain, no gain.

FIVE DEGREES OF SEPARATION

I'll be the first to value talent and experience over education. But let me stir the waters. For those with a degree, you can skip ahead. For those without a degree, let me persuade you to stop making excuses and get back to school. Although not always popular, the fact is that possessing a degree provides separation and increases the likelihood of upward mobility and salary for those who so desire. Bill Gates and Mark Zuckerberg are walking proof to the contrary, but they are also outliers. So get back to school.

I was about to get my MBA when my favorite college professor pulled me aside. Dr. Drennen said MBAs were "a dime a dozen" and that I should get a unique degree that would set me apart. She helped persuade me by throwing in a graduate teaching assistantship and other incentives. With a baby at home and mounting expenses, I enrolled in Consumer Sciences (business from a consumer vantage point). As the university contracted from eleven colleges to eight, Consumer Sciences was pooled with four other orphan programs: Apparel Design, Merchandising, Interior Design and Housing. Preparing for graduation after one intense calendar year, the assistant of this newly formed division was unsure how the diplomas should read. Since I'd been required to take a class in each of the disciplines, I suggested it should reflect this. Sure enough, I was essentially conferred all five degrees. Just don't ask me to pick out your suits or decorate your home!

Are degrees themselves so important? I suppose you can argue that the answer is yes when it comes down to being a physician or nurse or engineer. Other times, the course content has little correlation with our eventual work or skill requirements or how well we perform. We all know people with lots of book smarts who can't find their car in the parking lot. I get that. But something of more fundamental value arises from obtaining a degree than just the diploma.

I entered college at seventeen. Completely clueless, I ended up with a 1.6 GPA my freshman year. While I had some modest grants and loans, I had to work my rear off to live. I was dirt poor. But I stuck to it. I learned how to study. I learned discipline. I learned budget. I learned goal setting. I learned achievement. My grades improved, and I graduated.

My first roommate was an Italian rocker from the Bronx. I was a shaved-head punk. Our suite mates were nerds and the guy across the hall a dork. Down the hall lived jocks and geeks with punch cards. Some students worked two jobs like me while others were on daddy's dole. We had drinkers and druggies representing every walk of life. You learned to survive and form partnerships.

Life became complex. Unplugged from home, on your own, mom not there to wake you up. You had to make tough choices on majors and classes. You had to multi-task, set priorities for studying, and balance all of that with a social life. You became immersed and familiar with management concepts as you used them to keep your schedule under control. Each decision helped you mature.

Few of us escape school without encountering unrealistic professors and drama over jobs and administration. We learn life is not fair. We learn to fight for ourselves. We develop confidence as we come face to face with politics and negotiate our way.

Between the varied undergraduate classes, and moreover as a graduate student, I was exposed to many new ideas, concepts and experiences. Whether working with lab rats (in a clandestine early morning operation, I rescued my albino and set him free) or studying business, computers, poetry, design, etc., I was exposed to a world I would never otherwise have had the freedom or time to explore.

I have an open door policy and the welcome mat is worn. A common question I'm asked revolves around degrees. *Should I go back to school, and if yes, which degree to pursue?* My answer to the first part is almost always, yes! You learn much more than the degree content itself and it opens up doors for advancement. The type of degree depends on career goals and long-range objectives, but you can hardly go wrong with an undergraduate degree in business or a related field. For post-graduate work, I often recommend an MBA or MHA. No matter what, a safe bet is to follow your passion, even if the degree doesn't seem to fit. I once had a history major run my data centers well. My "5-degrees-in-1" has nothing to do with IT.

My mom never completed her secondary schooling because of the bombs that rained over southern Germany during World War II. She obtained her GED, enrolled in community college and graduated the same year I graduated from high school. My dad's schooling was short-circuited by his unique circumstances. But when he retired from the Army, and despite seven of us kids still at home, he jumped in and obtained a business degree before starting his second career.

I know many people have tough circumstance that might keep them from getting their degrees. Kids, time—all the pressures of the day job. It may need to wait a couple more years. But for others, you need a kick in the pants. I hope that after reading this, you'll explore your options again. Don't let pride interfere. Don't get hung up on the specific degree to get. This is a great opportunity for self-evaluation and reflection. Jump in and separate yourself.

BURN THE RÉSUMÉ

Unlike Hillary Clinton's infamous visit circa 1996, I landed in Kosovo during a period of relative calm. We flew in an unmarked military aircraft that was appointed more like a corporate jet than government transport. Despite the sight of armed soldiers, we had no fear of danger. Coming off the plane we were greeted by a chiseled young army sergeant, Jeff Masters. "Welcome to Kosovo Ma'am, Sir," which he then punctuated with a crisp salute.

A month prior, I received a call from the Army. I feared the worst. My Deputy CIO, Mike, had been activated to Kosovo as part of an aviation mission. To my great relief, he was fine. So why the call? Christmas was approaching, and the Army asked me to join generals, politicians and business leaders on a trip to encourage troops stationed in Kosovo. I had resigned my officer commission five years earlier, and the opportunity to spend time with troops again was a special honor.

Our roles had reversed, and my deputy was now in charge. He took me out in a don't-ask-for-permission, lights-out fly-by-terrain excursion in his Blackhawk helicopter. What a rush. Mike pushed the envelope trying to make me sick. Surprisingly, I did not pay a deposit to my barf bag. If I had, I would've never lived it down.

Sergeant Masters, the soldier who initially greeted us, was assigned as our escort to make sure we got from point A to point B without getting lost or killed. He went out of his way to make sure our party was comfortable, answered all our questions and showed us where the mess hall and latrine were. He was polished, confident, and his passion for service was evident. In fact, that first evening we observed an award ceremony where Sergeant Masters was decorated for superior performance. Generals sang his praises. I knew instantly I wanted this man to work for me when he left the service.

Sergeant Masters, a combat medic, had no technical experience. Before active duty he was a carpenter's apprentice. I didn't care, because he possessed what couldn't be taught: a passion for service and superior leadership. He, like anyone else, could learn IT. My convictions grew stronger as the week progressed. Once discharged from active duty, Jeff Masters brought his talent to my IT division.

I'm not big on résumés or the typical prerequisites. In the struggle to land my first "professional" job, I kept hearing recruiters cite my lack of experience or targeted education. Although I knew I could do the job, I could never break through. I was equipped with a master's degree and modest experience, but moreover, a passion to move mountains. Growing up, a huge chore list and having to pay my own way through college had built in me a hearty work ethic. I had the goods for success yet could not get my foot in the door. I was frustrated.

When I did enter the workforce, I found little correlation between experience and education, and actual performance. Ideally, you seek a high performer with requisite degrees and experience. But by no means is a robust résumé a guarantor of success. I owe my career acceleration to leaders who embraced the talent philosophy. Each took what traditional managers perceive as a great risk and offered me opportunities for which I did not "qualify." I'm forever grateful to my "connecters" Mary, Mike and Kevin. My journey brought clarity and success to my own recruiting and hiring decisions. Time taught me that the key to good hiring is spotting talent which, for me, meant spotting the naturally reoccurring behaviors and thought patterns of a champion. I'll take talent over years of service or education any day.

Nine months after Kosovo, we assigned Jeff Masters to manage a challenging project that was disorganized and poorly led. A year later the project successfully wrapped and yielded the promised benefits. Working closely with our technical division, Jeff learned field engineering skills and took a leadership role. Next, he joined the application team and learned CPOE (Computerized Physician Order Entry). There, he brought enthusiasm and organization to the team. He was then selected as the IT manager for coordinating the technology of a new hospital construction effort. The hospital opened on time and on budget and is serving its community today.

What a joy it is so see Jeff flourish, leveraging all his talents and continuously learning new skills. I have every expectation that this apprentice carpenter/combat medic will continue to hone his skills and achieve great things for those whom he serves. He has since begun work on his master's degree, but that's just window dressing for someone who's already a talented and highly competent professional.

Burn the résumé. Hire talent.

Glorious Mashup!

A common question I'm asked, and I suspect it is true of all leaders, is how I come up with a constant flow of ideas on innovation, leadership, business and clinical strategy, creativity, application.

The (short) safe answer: I'm not sure.

The (long) theoretical answer: The stuff I take in gets glomped by other intake and existing information which generate fresh perspectives. My mind is a mashup.

According to Wikipedia, the IT definition of a mashup is "a web application that combines data from more than one source into a single integrated tool." The example used is "the use of cartographic data from Google Maps to add location information to real estate data, thereby creating a new and distinct web service that was not originally provided by either source."

Mashup originally referred to the practice in pop music (notably hip-hop) of producing a new song by mixing two or more existing pieces together. Gwen Stefani is a good example of an artist who makes creative use of mashup with songs such as "Rich Girl" and "Wind it Up." Adam and the Ants did the same thing decades earlier by combining African drum rhythms with punk to help define their sound. Perhaps we can credit Bach as the original orchestrator with "St. Anne" in E-flat Major where he mashed up a triple fugue.

To enable a personal mashup, you need to be well rounded and have multiple input sources. Lessons learned as a young Army officer studying engineering concepts continue to influence my present intakes. My experience working with clinicians prior to my technology baptism was foundational. Thanks to earlier mentors, I established a career-long study of business. I've devoured hundreds of books to enrich my formal education. I feast weekly on a range of newspapers and magazines, most of them outside of healthcare and technology. I harvest inspiration from my external passions—family, faith, tango, music and athletics—that each add uniquely to my portfolio of intake and experience. The breadth and depth of my mashup is exponentially improved by engaging with individuals who possess a diverse set of experiences.

Mashups are rarely intentional. Most often they're happenstance. Imagine if all your staff were active individually and corporately as a mashup. Think of the collective potential. One way we encourage this phenomenon is by investing heavily in training. We complement this training with voluntary in-office book studies. During the first six months we used these studies at my organization, we have taught more than ten books, *none* of which were technical. Several were on leadership, a couple dipped into creativity, and the remaining explored service, business, and change.

"Rick's Library" is the brainchild of one of our analysts who has donated his office space for a library where anyone can check out tapes, CDs and books of all sorts. The intent is to encourage creativity and increase the opportunity for exposure to ideas. More people are beginning to think outside of IT parameters and add experiences and wisdom to form their own mashup. It's fun!

So don't just read about this. Apply it personally. Start by making a list of things you want to accomplish before you die to stretch yourself and your mind. Climb Mt. Kilimanjaro. Personally feed orphans in Guatemala. Swim the English Channel. Learn a foreign language. Dance on top the Eifel Tower. Go hang gliding. Read the Bible. Hike the Napali Coast. Glean wisdom from your grandmother. Become a Big Brother/Sister. Play games with your family. And for Pete's sake, stop wasting hours in front of the TV!

Do you want a never-ending flow of new ideas? The more diverse your collection of experience and input and the more people involved in the same will determine the rate at which you create mashups.

As Nike put it, "Just Do It!"

CIO reDefined: Chief Ironman Officer

The roles of a CIO are as varied as the companies and sectors they serve. Even within these roles are multiple combinations and permutations that are expressed according to circumstance. The moniker "CIO" itself is not limited to "Chief Information Officer." No, to be effective in our calling we must stretch the traditional definition beyond this commonly accepted interpretation. I've pushed the boundaries of conventional thinking surrounding the role. Here's why CIO also means "Chief *Ironman* Officer."

A photo I previously used as my avatar melds two of my passions: delivering technology innovations to improve the patient experience, and triathlon. In the foreground of the photo is my laptop. In the background is my tri-bike with associated gear. My dress is a mix of business and triathlon attire. Needless to say, the typical business picture idea bored me.

The avatar's conception is rooted in my Army Basic Training at Fort Dix, New Jersey in 1982. Despite my varsity high school accomplishments and the recruiter's assurances, I failed the Army Physical Fitness Test. I lacked the strength to perform the requisite push-ups, sit-ups, and run. Humiliated, I promised myself that I *would* pass the final test. I decided right then to never let anything I had complete control over compromise my ability to influence.

In the end, I passed. From that point forward, I consistently ranked with the top one percent of American soldiers in fitness and I maintained that for the rest of my military career.

Because of my avid enjoyment of sports, not to mention my early Army failure, I pushed my son too hard to "be like dad." As a result, he not only rebelled but maneuvered down the fast track to obesity. As an overweight middle schooler, he found team sports unpalatable—too much mocking and ostracizing. Thus, we toyed with multi-sports like triathlons, biathlons and duathlons. A short time later he would become a routine podium finisher and eventually he ranked fourth nationally for his age in duathlons. Our entire family had gotten involved, winning numerous races. My son and I in particular were hooked and have completed over fifty sport events since then, including two half-Ironman events in 2007 alone.

A full Ironman competition did not initially make it onto my list of objectives. When a friend of mine was suddenly diagnosed with cancer, I elected to battle the cause with her in my own way. All my training was carried out in honor and support of her fight. My time logged in preparation was sprinkled liberally with prayer for her and for the clinicians and researchers, that a cure might be found. In grooming for the Ironman (April 2008), I completed my first marathon in December 2007 in 3 hours and 43 minutes. That's a lot of prayer sprinkles.

While I am not advocating that every CIO should become an Ironman, I want to illuminate the profound lessons that apply to our profession:

- **Training.** Many CIOs believe no further training is necessary once they have reached the top. To the contrary, the requirements only increase with elevation. Continually equip yourself or you'll end up being removed from the race for taking up precious space. Like riding a bike, you can coast for a little bit but if you stop peddling, you will fall over.

- **Shape.** To the extent it is medically possible, stay in shape. The people you lead take their cues from you. Leaders bear the burden of visibility. Would you go to a pulmonologist who smokes? Or an orthodontist with crooked teeth? Studies have proven a correlation between physical and mental fitness. CIOs work long hours, which requires great stamina. You don't have to be an Ironman, but I encourage you to, at a minimum, follow the fitness recommendations of the American Heart Association.

- **Embrace change.** During triathlons, a racer faces many unforeseen circumstances. A strong wind. High tide. Or worse, a flat tire. No one is exempt from these trials. Do you accept the change and make the most of it, or do you spend energy fighting the elements you cannot control? Adapt to the curveballs thrown your way, and then thrive.

- **Guts.** It's not merely the most fit who win Ironman competitions. It's those who are fit *and* who want to win. Crave it. I have surpassed colleagues in my career who were much brighter than I, but they had neither the fortitude nor the focus to push through all the challenges. Painful things happen that will tempt you to quit. Develop and harness the power of passion, for passion will create guts and drive your success.

- **Boundaries expanded.** Early on, a 10K seemed like the ultimate race, an Olympic challenge. I never imagined attempting a marathon. Today, a 10K is a walk in the park. Ironman is busting the boundaries I originally believed invincible. As a CIO, you must continuously bust boundaries lest your organization becomes complacent, your vision dimmed and potentially lost.

- **Planning.** No one simply wakes up and decides to do an Ironman that morning. It takes advanced planning and years of transformational steps to see grand visions achieved. You must plan similarly for your career and your organization, analyzing both from short-term and long-term points of view. No greater sensation will seize you than when you see a plan fully executed and realized. It will fuel you to carry the journey into the future.

- **Rest and refueling.** There is a science to Ironman which includes rest and refueling. Continuous activity leads to burnout. If you do not take the time for nourishment you will run out of energy, perhaps even collapse. Constant action is not synonymous with effective action any more than eating junk food is nourishing. Build in time for rest and refueling.

Some may scoff at how, and why, I have portrayed the Chief Ironman Officer. Others will complain about the limitations, physical or otherwise, and to why this post is irrelevant. Yet thinking back, I recall events in which the blind, the aged, amputees, and even a quadriplegic passed me on a course and by their example I was encouraged to keep going.

I never thought I would say it, but I am thankful for my experiences as a seventeen-year-old basic trainee and for Drill Sergeant Moultrie screaming at me to eek out yet another push-up and run another lap. It is not so much about the physical act that inspired me but the leadership insights I internalized. Little did he realize the impact he would have on my life and career.

Or did he? Thank you, Sergeant Moultrie.

Now, get out there and race!

CHIEF *IRONMAN* OFFICER UPDATE:
LEADERSHIP LESSONS LEARNED FROM CHAMPIONS

At the time I wrote this, I was thirty days out from my first Ironman competition. I am a mix of nerves, enthusiasm and fear. Am I fit enough? Have I trained enough? What if I get injured before race day? What if I miss the swim cutoff time? (I'm a snail swimmer.) What if I flat more than twice? What if…?

Why am I doing this?

To facilitate my training and to familiarize myself with the race course, I attended a "multisport" camp. The camp was run by former professional athletes who had organized many Ironman events. One of them, Paula Newby-Fraser, had won 26 Ironman titles including eight world championships. At that time,

Paula had recorded the fastest finish among women. My first day at camp, I ran a warm-up 5K with her and gleaned all the wisdom possible regarding the course, the Ironman and running in general.

After an initial day of a short run, a short bike, and a long swim, we settled down for a hearty dinner. Camp leaders announced the cycling ride groups for the next day, which were formed based upon predicted finish times. I was selected to be in the fastest group led by the number one ranked woman Ironman in the world. Fear struck me like a bolt of lightning, and I considered putting myself in a slower group. Michellie Jones, "Miss Number One Ironman" (my nickname for my assigned group leader), happened to be sitting across from me at dinner. I promptly confessed, "I can probably hold my own cycling at twenty mph for five hours, but that's my max."

She no doubt heard the fear in my voice, yet still replied, "You'll be fine with that."

I didn't believe her.

She added, "I like to start off slow and finish fast."

God save me!

Apprehensive about the ride, I woke up three times that night. I wanted to drop to a slower group, and yet I couldn't shrink from the challenge. Finally, I decided if I got dropped I'd just slow down and wait for the other ride groups to catch up.

That sounded like a reasonable backup plan until my ride group gathered that morning. Of the ten riders, five were professionals; of the other five—mortals like me—I was the only "virgin" Ironman. Talk about a clay blob among marble statues. Their bikes and aerodynamic outfits were three times as costly as mine was, and I was the only soft body amongst hard bodies. This was going to be a long day.

We set off at a blistering 26-mph pace. Despite a fitful sleep, I had fairly fresh legs and was able to stay steady for the first 40 miles. In search of hills, we headed off the Ironman course and found some rollers with lengthy inclines. We had already lost two mortals; I was determined not to be the third. I was sixth in the draft line, and I noticed the cyclist in front of me falling off the pace, which meant I was falling off the peloton as well. At first, it was just a couple yards, but that stretched to ten yards, and I knew we were in trouble. We wouldn't be able to push back up to the pack.

Lesson 1: Be sure the person you are following has the vision and stamina to keep you on the straight and narrow. "Followership" is a critical talent for survival.

The turnaround point for our hill excursion was coming up, and I managed to get back in the line. I understood clearly that the key to my survival was drafting closely, if not right behind the leader, in this case Michellie, "Miss Number One". I stayed slightly to her left with my front wheel overlapping her rear wheel by an inch or two. I drafted well and during this stretch at about 28 mph, I was smiling, having the ride of my life. I was drafting behind the world's best! My legs felt fresh again, and my confidence reawakened. About mile 80, we started to hit a gradual incline. As the last surviving mortal, I slipped to third position, then fourth, and was soon passed by the peloton. Heading up the incline, they stayed steady at 25 mph, but I was too far off to draft. I ended up facing the wind resistance alone. Despite increased physical effort and motivation, my speed dropped to 18 mph. I was alone in the desert. I could do nothing in my own power to reach them.

Lesson 2: Riding in a pack you can gain 40 percent efficiencies over riding alone. Teams can accomplish more. Pushing and pulling together, a team outperforms the loner every time.

A few miles down the road, I was saved by the refueling vehicle that carried extra drinks and food. As we resumed, I took second position behind Michellie and did not let go. I was smiling again. No more inclines, all flat terrain. The closer together we rode in the peloton, the greater the "eddy" we produced, which helped propel Michellie forward. It was a truly symbiotic endeavor. As we reached the mile 90, however, I was riding on empty, and Michellie razzed me for the umpteenth time about inadequate hydration. She made me a concoction out of two of her bottles, and we finished in a flourish. By the time we coasted into the finish lot, I was cracking up. I had just ridden over 100 miles with *the* Michellie Jones. And this woman led no patsy ride!

Lesson 3: Sometimes it takes sheer grit and hunger, but you can push yourself to do amazing things. Test your boundaries, then break through and grow to the next level. Just do it!

Throughout the camp, someone kept saying, "It's about performance, baby!" One definition of performance: the efficiency with which something fulfills its intended purpose.

Last year's trophy looks nice on the shelf. I have a few of my own, including work-related awards. But their beauty is fleeting. Their intended purpose has stagnated. Sitting back and bragging about yesteryear's accomplishments is fruitless, inefficient. At some point, the past no longer matters. It is about what you're going to do in the next race. Sponsors aren't seeking out racers because they were yesterday's champ or because they'd been doing Ironman for 20 years. They're searching for the continuous quality, or excellence, of a racer—the guy who keeps pushing himself to perform and improve. The same should hold true in our healthcare careers.

Lesson 4: You can coast for only so long in the draft of a trophy, but when you cease pedaling, you will fall over.

I'll wrap this up with bullets of wisdom gleaned from champions:

- Teamwork
- Followership
- Sheer grit
- Breakthrough
- Performance
- Even gifted leaders need a coach

See you at the finish line!

11

VOLUNTEER AND
GIVE UNTIL IT HURTS

vol • un • teer (vol′ən tēr), n.
1. a person who voluntarily offers himself or herself for a service or undertaking. 2. a person who performs a service willingly and without pay.

Open Arms Clinic team on opening day. Tanzania, June 2011

Volunteering keeps you grounded. It enables humility. It also creates additional opportunities for a variety of inputs into your life that can stimulate creativity.

For five years, every Wednesday, I worked as a volunteer in one of our health centers. Sometimes I would do it with my son. The great thing about it was I got to see patients and understand and empathize with them.

When you volunteer, it opens your eyes and connects you to the world around you in ways that you are not used to. It makes you vulnerable, sure, but it also enriches you and makes you feel like you are truly contributing. It goes back to humility. Makes you more humble. It's good to give of yourself.

Give until it hurts. It is through that hurt, that suffering, that we build character.

GRILLED CHEESE SANDWICH, PLEASE

As a new CIO, I spent the first five years volunteering after hours for our health system. They assigned me to the greatest volunteer opportunity available. Each Wednesday afternoon, I went room-to-room delivering $10 gift shop vouchers to all the winners of our closed circuit TV bingo game. Bingo was the highlight of the week for hundreds of patients and their families. The game normally finished around 4 p.m. I'd pick up the certificates at 5 p.m. and hand-deliver them to the winners.

While striving to take our IT shop from bad to good, I was not always Mr. Popular with my customers. Thus, volunteering became the highlight of my week. It got me out of the office and into our hospitals. Everyone wanted to see me. Everyone welcomed me. Wednesday evenings became a salubrious respite from the work grind I faced the rest of the week.

Observing joy in the recipients' faces brought my heart pleasure. Think about it. These citizens were stuck in a hospital; receiving a voucher for a $10 credit at the gift shop meant everything. And their responses had an impact on me. I stopped taking life for granted and started embracing the simple things.

Volunteering routinely also broke my heart, especially those dreaded deliveries to the fifth floor of our children's hospital. As I scrubbed in before entering the floor, I took twice as long to wash in an attempt to delay the inevitable—I was about come face-to-face with kids the same age as mine, except these children were dying. I'd knock gently on the door, and they would be looking right at me. Expectant. Picturing my own two children in their situation, I'd swallow hard and muster up a smile. But then the joy in these young patients' faces made the sorrow worthwhile. Before leaving the floor, I'd stop in the restroom and let my smile fade to a cry.

I learned the value of listening. When I delivered vouchers to the elderly, they always wanted to chat. They cared more about having company and far less about the vouchers. Oh, the loneliness I witnessed! As much as I wanted to hurry these interactions and get on to the next winner, I envisioned my own parents and thought how I would love for someone to spend time with them if I could not be there. I met many interesting characters. The love I saw between seasoned married couples encouraged me in my marriage. I recall one man holding the hand of his sickly wife. The lines in their faces proved a beautiful testimony of a life well lived and a true commitment through health and sickness.

I'll never forget the mom who met me in the pediatric ICU waiting room. Before I could reach her child's room, she said, "Can I use the voucher in the cafeteria?" Although the vouchers were strictly for the gift shop, I took her down there to see what we could negotiate. She went to the grill and asked for a grilled cheese sandwich. "We don't serve grilled cheese sandwiches," the cook said. The exasperated mother all but begged. "My daughter just woke up from months in a coma, and her first words were, 'Mommy I'm hungry, I want a grilled cheese sandwich.'" *Tissue please.* The cook made the off-menu grilled cheese sandwich while the woman wept.

Ask anyone who knows me, and they'll tell you—often with a shudder—that I'm a Type-A personality. My wife tells me I'm an extremist—all or nothing. I am wired to compete—and win. I can't climb just any mountain, I have to summit the highest peaks—all of them. Army combat training taught me to kill with my hands, and my kids say when I'm overly focused on a project I look ticked off at the world (I'm not really, and I'm working on smiling more). But volunteering became my counterbalance. Interacting with the sick, feeble, and dying helped shave the edge off my hardcore design.

What keeps you balanced? When you see a bed of roses, do you stop to enjoy their scent? Or does just the thought of pausing to take in the "life" happening around you ruffle your nerves?

I miss bingo. I miss weekly interactions with patients. Those memories still stick with me. The emotions still live vividly. I'm ready to jump back in and refresh the experience.

Grilled cheese anyone?

GIVING AWAY OUR CHRISTMAS

We have always worked hard as a family to serve and give to others. For a couple of years, when our kids were teenagers, we as a family decided to pool all of the money we would have spent on each other for Christmas and put that money toward some really meaningful act of giving.

We all had what we needed; we knew that we were immensely blessed. So, instead of all of the gifts under the Christmas tree, we tallied all that money up and we looked around for a meaningful, significant gift that would help people who really needed it. We found this organization that had a number of these gifts available—for example, if you gave a certain amount it might mean shelter for a family for a year, provide them with or medical supplies, things like that.

We sat together as a family and decided to pool our gift money together—I think it was around a couple of thousand dollars—and we "gave away" our Christmas. I talk a lot about giving until it hurts, and truthfully this kind of giving does hurt in ways. Our family loves Christmas; we love the Christmas tree, the spirit of the season and the tradition of giving gifts to each other on Christmas Eve.

We agreed no presents that year, just a symbolic present under the tree representing the bigger gift we had given to those who really needed it.

Think about the bigger picture. Give away your Christmas. Give until it hurts.

A NEW COAT FOR CHRISTMAS

One of the most incredible stories I remember from volunteering is from our days in Cleveland and the Friday nights our church would do a mobile soup kitchen. We would go out and serve hot food to homeless people. We would also hand out toiletries and other supplies—whatever had been donated.

We would also always offer to pray for people. We wouldn't push it, but most of the time people were receptive to it. This one time, it was September or October and starting to get cold. We asked this man—an African American guy—if there was something we could pray for and he said "I really need a winter coat. It's really getting cold."

This woman started praying for him to have a new winter coat. Most of the time we prayed generically, not for a specific item or action. But this woman is praying for this man to have a new winter coat right now. So we finished praying and I turned away to talk to someone behind me and when I turned back around the homeless man is standing there with a new coat! He had this huge smile on his face and he was wearing this new winter coat.

Talk about an extraordinary story! It turns out, and this is a great example of how I believe God works, while we were praying, there was another woman from our team walking by. She heard the guy asking so sincerely for a new winter coat. And she remembered that she had just bought her husband a new winter coat and it was in the car. She went to the car and brought it to him...

If you don't volunteer, you don't experience these kinds of extraordinary tales.

Vacations With A Purpose

For years my wife and I have been involved in mission trips—visits to places where people are less fortunate than we are—with the goal of serving them and making their lives perhaps a bit easier. More recently, we came upon the idea of formally combining vacation and mission trips—vacations with a purpose.

It's so easy to get caught up in our own lives in our own world. We get in the mindset of wanting more things, newer things. We have found that even taking a few days per year and visiting a disadvantaged country to see how the rest of the world lives can not only be a great way to give back, but also be reminded of just how great we have it here in the United States—how blessed we truly are.

There are organizations that set up these vacations with a purpose. We worked with one such organization, CompassioNet, to take a missionary vacation in Puerto Vallarta, Mexico, with our two then teenaged children. It was an amazing trip. We not only enjoyed the rest and relaxation one hopes to achieve on vacation, but we were able to visit some truly impoverished villages filled with the most amazing people. It was humbling to realize how much we have when we see how little they survive on.

For us as a family—and as individuals—this kind of trip is a great way to reset and ground ourselves. And from the standpoint of our children who grow up in this society wanting for almost nothing, they get a real world perspective on how other people live in not so fortunate parts of the world. It's truly eye-opening for them. They see children who literally have nothing except the clothes on their backs. It helps our kids really appreciate what they have and to not take their lives for granted. We spent most of our time with the "dump families." Families that literally live on an ever growing mountain of garbage. They scavenge every day for food and supplies while competing with giant vultures.

Our kids were 16 and 12 respectively when we first took them on a mission trip. It was extremely impactful for them. It has really made a difference in their upbringing. We ended up taking four or five of these trips over the years. I fully expect them to go on their own mission trips as adults, hopefully with their own families.

Truthfully, you do not need to leave this country or travel far to find your own missionary vacations. There are many opportunities to serve and have an impact on those less fortunate than you very close to home. You can feed the homeless, you can perform random acts of service, or if it suits you, you can take the kind of mission vacations we have. It really does allow you to get away from your daily lives and make a difference in this world at the same time.

It's so important to get out beyond yourself. The more you can do that, the more you can do for others, the more extraordinary experiences you will have.

12

BUILD STRONG IDENTITY

i • den • ti • ty (i den'ti tē), n.
1. the state or fact of remaining the same one or ones, as under varying aspects or conditions: *The identity of the fingerprints on the gun proved he was the killer.* 2. the sense of self, providing sameness and continuity in personality over time.

4 generations of Marx men, L-R Herbert, Edward, Britton and Brandon

You must know who you are.

I don't think most people do. Most people's identity is based on accolades, trophies. Many people look for external affirmation to create their identity. What happens if those stop coming?

Knowing yourself keeps you from falling into a false sense of who you are and what is important. Knowing yourself breeds the confidence required to live life congruent with your values and not compromising core beliefs.

Strong identity shelters you from the inevitable pain and destruction when we live life inconsistently.

Zig Ziglar said "Attitude not aptitude determines altitude."

Who are you? It's a process that you must go through.

IDENTITY AND THE LEADER

I vividly recall at age seventeen, jumping off the bus at the in-processing station of Fort Dix, New Jersey, where a drill sergeant greeted me—screaming.

By the third day, I wore a uniform, had a shaved head, and was organized into a squad and a platoon.

The drill sergeant shouted, "Look to your left and look to your right and now look down at yourself. In nine weeks, one of you will not be here because you do not have what it takes to be a United States warrior!" *Gulp.* He scared the crap out of me. But looking around, I determined I was better than at least one or two of my fellow trainees. Yep, I would be okay.

A couple of weeks after I graduated as Private Marx, I entered freshman orientation at Colorado State University as a poster child for insecurity. I have no recollection of who spoke that day, but I do remember the speaker saying that 80,000+ students had graduated in the past 100 years. I pondered the odds and decided, **Surely, there were other bozos like me who made it, so I too can succeed.**

Since childhood, the comparison method had been a pervasive mindset for me. My identity had been in *what* I was rather than *who* I was. And I'd based my success on *what* I could create rather than *why* I had been created. I floundered under that junior high mentality of "I am significant because *you* are less significant." This warped attitude gave me a false confidence in the workplace. I'd compared myself to my peers and to those above me. Sometimes I would try to learn from others who were stronger and smarter than I, but more often than not, I would pounce on their weaknesses to climb over them and up the career ladder. Sure, my skills and talents have helped boost my success, but I was also counterfeiting my identity and confidence based on others' deficiencies and weaknesses.

Leaving that mindset behind, I was searching for the real me and trying to live as the "Genuine Ed"—insecurity surrendering to conviction.

After qualifying for the USA National Championship Duathlon (run-bike-run) as an average athlete, I had just hoped to finish the darned race. Qualifying for a spot on Team USA was not only about to become a dream come true but also a test of my desire to be the genuine Ed.

At first, I suffered second thoughts based on my insecurities. The odds for success were not in my favor. In fact, competing at this elite level I'd likely end up embarrassing myself. But there I was already comparing myself again. Yet this was my only shot to compete with the gifted.

When I arrived in Tucson and began the registration process, I started doing what most athletes do—comparing myself to others. *That guy has less body fat.* Another athlete was clean-shaven all over. The guy next to him had a $10,000 bike. The woman in the corner was sponsored.... Pretty soon I stood there mentally defeated with the race a mere two days away. I was still basing my success on how I compared to others, not on who I was.

Damn that warped thinking! I stopped it and chose to walk in the opposite spirit. I decided that what I had—a strong heart, a decent bike, and an okay, albeit, hairy body—was sufficient. I chose to look forward and not to my right or left. The outcome wasn't in my hands anyway. As an athlete, what mattered was how will *my* stats in this performance compare to *my* stats in the previous races. Was I improving? Forget the guy racing next to me. If I was meant to represent Team USA at the 2014 World Championships, then that would happen.

Identity is a tricky thing. What is it? How is it formed? How does it impact who we are and our performance? Most of the time, I base my identity on how I believe I compare to others. I suspect most of us are miswired to think this way.

I don't claim to have it figured out; I've already proved that. My true identity is squaring who I was made to be and living congruently with this truth. I'm still working on it, but as I approached 50, I was finally getting close. If these ideas help nudge you in the right direction, I will have accomplished my goal for this post.

Some self-reflection ideas:

- Is my life/career mission about me, or about the betterment and growth of those around me?

- What do I stand for?

- Do my values reflect a desire to see others succeed, or do they revolve exclusively around my personal success?

- Does my behavior reflect a value for the human soul?

- What's my gauge for comparison: other people or stable virtues?

- Am I able to sincerely rejoice in others' accomplishments, or do I have to one-up people all the time?

- Do I go to bed praying that no one finds out how insecure I am?

Who are you really? And are you happy with you?

LEADERSHIP AND IDENTITY—I LOOK BETTER THAN YOU!

You might argue with where the identity journey has taken me, but the fact is, all of us have been a counterfeit to one degree or another.

Marx family portrait to include son Brandon, daughter Talitha, daughter in-law Nicole and grandson Britton. Colleyville, TX Sept 2013

Does how you see me agree with reality? Do I even know who I am? Really?

Janis Ian nailed me with her song "At Seventeen." Thank goodness I had a supportive family and a slight awareness of the love of our scandalous Creator because when I first moved to the United States as a preteen, I dressed unusually. Kids made fun of my traditional German attire. As I came of age, acne invaded my complexion, giving classmates another reason to pick on me. I never got the girls I crushed on. I was ostracized and spinning downward in self-hatred.

Rather than surrendering to a super low self-esteem funk that could self-imprison me for life, I fought for validation and identity via sports. Continual reinforcement from adults and peers convinced me that success on the playing field signified acceptance and popularity. Where a lack of clear-skinned attractiveness had stolen my self-confidence, I made up for it through tennis and soccer. Sheer determination compensated for my skill deficiencies. My idolized letterman jacket became like pure gold to me and epitomized my counterfeit identity.

Sports accolades helped establish an achievement-based identity. Extreme achievements gave me a sugar-like high that would, in time, fuel my adult lifestyle. This placebo-based identity would affect my relationships, both personal and professional.

As I passed through college and into my career, the focus on looks became less important than champion skills. But the deceptive *ugly bug* still had a grip. I compared myself to other men. I poured significant energy and resource into making myself *look* better—excessive exercise, extreme diet, fine clothing, braces—anything to bury the insecurity.

My teeth! I had this Michael Strahan-sized gap between my front teeth, so I put myself through adult mini-hell—braces. The gap's gone now. But then they weren't white enough. So I got them whitened, and, lo and behold, I spotted someone with whiter teeth than mine. Ugh! A close friend complained that I was too hairy. So, what did I do? Yep, and after that painful process, the same friend said I was too white. Thankfully, I tumbled off the merry-go-round before the first tanning session. What the hell was I doing?

Insanity! I've even contributed to this appearance ruse! I recall the day some fool cut me off in traffic and almost got us in an accident. Cursing, I pulled up to the person to flip the bird. When I saw she was gorgeous, I just waved. I'm embarrassed to admit that, but I know I'm not alone. When people are given a choice between two candidates, most tend to choose the prettier person.

I'll never forget my final interview for a Fortune 50 management trainee program. I had made it to the final eight, four of whom would be selected for this prestigious position. The COO invited me into his office and dismissed my résumé and pat questioning as he said, "At this level, all candidates have the same background…a graduate degree, high aptitude and strong skills. So I just want to look at you." I was thinking, *shit, this interview is over.* Yep, I no longer "qualified" for the job.

Sure, it's healthy to maintain yourself, look your best, and especially to re-main attractive to your partner. But when we nail our identity to our frame and features, we have a major problem. Major! We all know people who are preoccu-pied with their mirrored reflection. Undoubtedly, as you age you'll be displaced by others more attractive. Neither time or gravity is on your side. If you try to compete, the amount of hours and dollars you spend on your looks will only in-crease. And in the end, guess what? Someone else will always be better looking. You'll never be satisfied! Or rewarded.

I've woken up from the Hollywood delusion.

As I have approached 50, here's what I'm learning. I need to get out of the false-identity trap that says my appearance is so grossly important. Yes, I do what I can to take care of myself, but I will no longer be excessive. Here are a couple of self-tests:

- If a flare up of acne determines whether you have a good or bad day, take a time out.

- If you're more concerned about people liking your new hair-style and less concerned about your own derogatory comments to others, you have an issue.

The good news is that we can overcome. I am learning to accept myself as I've been created. I was meant to be 5'8" so I embrace that height. If my genes say I'm balding, I'll stop the ridiculous comb-over. If I am hairy then… well, okay, I have to draw the line somewhere. ☺

Here's the deal. Allowing shallow people and a fluctuating society to determine my identity creates a "lose-lose" situation. My identity stems from what's inside me. Character triumphs over a perfect nose job. This cultural issue is nothing new. Two-thousand years ago, wise men said:

> "What matters is not your outer appearance—the styling of your hair, the jewelry you wear, the cut of your clothes—but your inner disposition."

> "We should be concerned most with the transformation of the inner man, not outward appearances…."

Traits that are skin-deep are not worth obsessing over or bragging about. If you're so vain you think this post is about you, it's not. It me spilling my guts. But if you're honest enough to admit to feeling pain while reading this, we might share a common struggle. Our value reaches much deeper.-

As a leader on the slippery slope, where are you investing your time, money, and effort? In someone who is skin-deep, or in the real you?

LEADERSHIP AND IDENTITY—IT'S ALL ABOUT THE TITLE!

In our office lobby display case, the theme of the month was "pets." One of my associates, David, had a picture of his beautiful hunting dog, but what caught my eye was the castle ruin in the background. "Oh, that's Bective Abbey, right across the street from my parents' home in Meath. The remaining cloisters were used in scenes from *Braveheart*." Jokingly, I said, "Beautiful. Let's go." Four weeks later David and I were standing in the actual spot, walking the castle ruins. Although the movie *Braveheart* was about Scotland, many of the movie shots took place in Ireland, in David's backyard. So to prepare ourselves, we watched the movie three or four times.

Braveheart is full of leadership lessons but the following interchange between Robert the Bruce and William Wallace stuck with me.

Robert the Bruce: "I'm not a coward. I want what you want, but we need the nobles."

William Wallace: "We need them?"

Robert the Bruce: "Aye."

William Wallace: "Nobles. Now tell me, what does that mean to be noble? Your title gives you claim to the throne of our country, *but men don't follow titles, they follow courage.* Now our people know you. Noble, and common, they respect you. And if you would just lead them to freedom, they'd follow you. And so would I."

The same is true in life. Screw the title, focus on leadership. Title holds significance when it's earned through performance.

People want to follow leaders, not titles.

Look at the 2013 Time Magazine Man of the Year, Pope Francis. Did Francis suddenly transform into a unique leader because he became Pope? No! If you know his history as a Cardinal and Archbishop, nothing he does as Pope should surprise you. Did he become Pope because he sought a title? That he is often called "the reluctant Pope," tells us that seeking a title was not on his goal sheet. Serving people had *always* taken precedence.

I am not naïve to suggest this is always the case. We know plenty of people who gained titles by stepping on others—a Machiavellian, winning-at-all-costs approach. But I can tell you, the most successful leaders never sought titles, they sought to humbly serve. The former are easy to spot and do not get enough respect.

One of my directors, I'll call her Tracy, was a damn good analyst. She didn't seek a title, she just pursued her role and responsibility with vigor. She accomplished great things, and we gave her more. We saw the results and potential so we promoted her to a director, and she has been awesome.

In another instance, I was struggling to fill our chief security officer role. One day, I asked a recently retired Marine what his defining moment was. He described how, as a staff sergeant, he stood down a full-bird colonel. You see, he cared about doing the right thing despite anyone's title. That's moxie. It's leadership. I hired him on the spot. You think he will stand down from an executive or his manager if our security posture is compromised. Never! Title is secondary to effective leaders.

Do you possess your title or does it possess you?

A good test: Do you ever use your title to get things done or get your way? I rarely refer to myself as senior vice president or CIO. When I am in meetings I tell people I serve as a leader in leveraging technology to enable superior business and clinical outcomes. I do what I can to not to let title get to my head. Humility is the key. Watch for the slippery slope. It will take your title and life if you are not careful. I know.

Much of what I'm writing is logical and intuitive but not often practiced. We are driven and ambitious and we seek instant gratification. We toiled well for a few months so we think we deserve that next promotion. But I tell you the truth, gaining titles before you are prepared is very dangerous to both you and your organization. Stop the pursuit. Focus on being the best at whatever you do. The rest will follow.

Some of you are thinking, *Ed I do all that…I don't seek crowns. I seek to serve, and the title never comes. In fact, I see others being promoted over me that offer half the value I do.* I get it. It happens. The world is not fair. Continue to work your ass off and double down on your efforts. Find other ways to increase your value to the organization. Expand. Ask for more responsibilities. Volunteer. But if at some point, over multiple years, you're doing all these things consistently and still nothing? Yep, time to bail.

Again, I'm a work in progress. Some of the things I write are aspirational for me. I struggle with the same things as you: pride, arrogance, achievement orientation and instant gratification. But I am slowly catching on to this identity thing. Taken me all of about fifty years. Hopefully it will stick for the next fifty.

Damn, this is easy to write but hard to internalize, yet it is the truth.

For me, identity is not rooted in title, looks or what I do. It is who I am and what I stand for, believe in, and practice. I am trying hard to forge my identity in my faith in God. I like the sound of CEO, but His title is what I desire. "I am free. I am new. I am a saint. I am alive. I am all He says I am. I am His own."

My detractors are right in the sense I fall short of the above list. However, only one opinion about me counts—and my detractors are not the One who matters.

LEADERSHIP AND IDENTITY—
LOOK AT ME! LOOK AT ME! LOOK AT ME!

We may not admit it, but most of us crave recognition and awards like a drug. Receiving honors gets us high. We love the buzz that says, "I'm better than you." Accolades, though fine on their own, can create an identity on which we base our self-esteem and worth. But it's only a short-term fix, and the satisfaction quickly fades. The buzz wears off. Worldly recognition is a pursuit that never quenches the real need for significance and worth. The new gold plaque merely masks our insecurities. So we seek after more, something bigger. Perhaps a more prestigious award. Another graduate degree. Another Fellowship.

Don't believe it? Search the thousands of companies out there that make a living off our need for recognition. Peruse the corporate office walls. Facebook screams, LOOK AT ME!

You want to score a quick hookup? Talk up your target and pour on verbal affirmation and validation. Want to watch a coward become a hero? Entice him with a ribbon for his chest. Humans are complex for sure, but when it comes to our ego's need for glory, we are singularly focused, simple minded, and easily led astray.

Hey, I'm stuck there too in the "Look at me!" frenzy. I have sacrificed those most important to me just to win that coveted award. I worked longer hours than reasonable just to be ranked number one. I had to add cabinets to store my prizes. Heck, I spent three hours per day in the gym purely so I could out-perform those half my age and get a medal around my neck to brag about it. I know I'm not alone. I've watched marriages destroyed because some guy needed to upgrade his trophy wife. It's madness! And I am determined to stop it in my own life.

Whoa, now, hold on a minute! There is nothing wrong with winning awards and being recognized for great service or whatever. True. But it becomes a problem when we make it the foundation for our identity. How do you know you have an identity issue? Ask yourself some key questions:

- Do you fee; defensive reading this so far?

- Do you perform so you can get your name engraved on a plaque?

- Do you covet the other guy's award?

- At parties, do you brag about your trophies, medals, certificates?

- When in conversation, can you draw out the success of others without speaking a word about your last honor?

- Do you set performance targets because they are the right thing to do or because they will gather positive self-attention?

- Who do your pursuits make more famous: your employer or you?

- When you receive recognition, do you take all the glory or share it?

- When you receive recognition, do you display false modesty?

- Do you live for yourself or for others?

- Do you always need to be in control?

- Are you constantly bewitched by the legacy you will leave?

- When you don't win what you want, are you ticked off?

If your identity is based on the need for external validation, what can you do? First, get rid of people who feed you bullshit. You know who they are" the ones who make you feel good because they inflate your ego. Replace them with people who will be brutally honest and have no fear of repercussion. How do you know who they are? They're the ones who make you mad. A couple of my direct reports are good at this. I have staffers who are unafraid of me and get in my face. I love 'em! If there is nobody close to you who challenges you to the point of making you mad, you might need an identity reboot. Conflict, not flattery, is what helps build our character.

So as I get older, I find myself on a new learning curve and, man, the growth is painful. I'm okay with recognition and awards now as long as they are purely an external validation of an internal (team) reality. I won't personally pursue them nor take actions for the sole purpose of personal fame. Finding my true self is painful and ugly, but at the same time, gloriously beautiful. And freeing.

I'll leave you with this from one of my heroes, Saint Paul:

> "The very credentials these people are waving around as something special, I'm tearing up and throwing out with the trash—along with everything else I used to take credit for. And why? Because of Christ. Yes, all the things I once thought were so important are gone from my life. Compared to the high privilege of knowing Christ Jesus as my Master, firsthand, everything I once thought I had going for me is insignificant—dog dung. I've dumped it all in the trash so that I could embrace Christ and be embraced by him."

An identity based on what you do, how you look, or your titles and awards, will not lead to fulfillment. What I'm learning is truth for me and it's rooted in faith. I know I am Edward Marx. A follower of Christ. Here to serve and point others towards the pursuit of truth. I might fail, but I will get back up and move forward.

Who are you? In what is your identity rooted?

THE GOOD BOSS

One of my assignments as a young captain in the Army Reserve was serving as the convoy commander for our combat engineer battalion. We were moving more than 250 vehicles across the state of Colorado. Given the size and type of vehicles (Hummers, dump trucks, semi-tractors carrying bulldozers), we covered a good fifteen miles of highway end to end. I missed a turn and inadvertently split my convoy in two. Applying a few off-road techniques within a couple hours I'd reassembled my convoy. But not before catching the attention of the Battalion Commander.

At our next stop, I steeled myself for one of the famous "ass chewings" our Commander was known for. We both stepped out of our Hummers and he looked at me and said, "Carry on Marx!" He spun back around and climbed into his vehicle. That was it. And you know what, for me that was all it took. And he knew it. He purposefully chose a different form of discipline for that situation. Later, he told me that he could tell by the look on my face that I had learned the lesson and understood the gravity. He did not have to say anything more. And he didn't. He was a Good Boss.

So what makes a Good Boss?

I don't believe there is a magical checklist of Good Boss attributes. There are too many variables and permutations. Put simply, the Good Boss first and foremost does not follow a checklist. He or she understands every person is unique and should be treated as such. Just like my Commander after my convoy fiasco.

I crowd sourced for input and here is a compilation of attributes of a Good Boss. This is not research or academia or consultant or stats based on one person's experience. It is not a checklist. These are ideas, and I imagine they reflect the thinking of your staff as well. Ponder the following and adopt as your situation dictates.

- Ensures Appreciation and Value
  - Says "thank you" regularly
  - Demonstrates gratitude in words and action and rewards success
  - Personalizes awards and recognition
  - Listens often
  - Gives you glory for success
- Mentoring
  - Takes active interest in your career and guides growth in the job
  - Teaches how to best interact with customers
  - Encourages professional development and provides educational opportunities
  - Willing to learn from you
  - Hopes one day you will step into his position
  - Guides you to your ultimate goal, even if it means losing you
- Fairness
  - Never steals ideas from their staff
  - Always honest with you and ethical to the core
  - Does not undermine anyone
  - Possesses a strong work ethic
  - Treats everyone without bias (race, religion, ethnicity, gender, age)

- Performance
    - Sets high but reasonable standards and removes non-performers
    - Gets more out of you than you can get from yourself
    - Sustains the continuity of the organization by only hiring "A" players
    - Provides insightful and regular feedback
    - Elevates your performance without you even noticing
    - Provides appropriate tools and training for the job
- Team
    - Holds individuals accountable to performance standards so team does not suffer
    - Represents team and department with passion and confidence
    - Makes you feel proud to be on the team
    - Takes public responsibility for the action of the team when failures occur
- Transparency
    - Makes themselves transparent and vulnerable
    - Admits errors and apologizes without excuse
    - Gets to know you as a person (family, hobbies)
    - In tune with their emotions and not afraid to show it (smile, laugh, cry)
    - Shares their wisdom in decision making and is open to other possibilities
- Vision
    - Encourages vision

- o Articulates and lives the mission and values of the organization
- o Tells you when to be practical and when to dream
- Positive
  - o Remains positive when things don't go as planned
  - o Always finds the good in bad situations
- Individuality
  - o Does not micromanage and allows for creativity and self-expression
  - o Welcomes and supports innovation and creativity
  - o Recognizes individual's strengths and positions people accordingly
  - o Knows when to be the boss, friend, or mentor
  - o Knows when to lighten difficult moments
- Style
  - o Leads by influence and not by position
  - o Jumps in the trenches with you as needed
  - o Walks the talk and shows flexibility
  - o Trusts and respects and gives benefit of the doubt
  - o Possesses high emotional and social intelligence

Is this how your staff describes you? Which of these attributes will strengthen your leadership? Remember, one size does not fit all. Treat everyone in the style that works best for that individual and circumstance.

Be the boss! The *good* boss.

THE BAD BOSS

New town. New job. I was stoked over what was essentially a start-up within an enterprise. As a visual learner and teacher, I asked the office manager for a whiteboard. No-go. The president wanted to keep corporate operating costs low. No worries, I went to Staples, and for the cost of a Starbucks Grande Red Eye, I bought myself a whiteboard.

Before I had a chance to hang my would-be art piece, my boss stopped in and frowned. "What's this?" After I explained my reasoning, he said, "Take it out." He wanted all the offices to have the same, minimalist look and feel.

Well, my kids loved it. That whiteboard became central to their home school activities. I've used it over the years for meetings at home.

Little did I know, the rejected whiteboard was only an omen of the legalistic reign under which I was now employed. I was tempted to pack up and head back south. After all, I had a 90-day "get-out-of-jail-free" card from my former employer who would graciously welcome me back. Our old home had not yet sold.

Tempted as I was to escape, I knew running away was wrong. If I quit then, I would never learn perseverance. I had made a commitment and I would keep it, no matter how aggravating. I knew I would use this challenging experience to prepare for the future. Angry and disillusioned, I stuck it out.

Most of us have had a manager who's aggravated the heck out of us. National employee engagement scores from Gallup suggest many are presently in such situations. Websites such as Really Bad Boss (www.reallybadboss.com) are extremely popular. Numerous best-sellers have been written on the subject. And did you ever ask yourself why *The Office* and *Dilbert* are such big hits? Because we can all relate on some level to bad bosses. I suspect all of us will have the opportunity to encounter one along the way. This was mine.

I make an effort to understand these concerns because I don't want to be a *bad boss*. And I'm very aware of my potential to become what I hate. We're all susceptible.

That said, I've been blessed to work with predominantly good bosses. So here is what I learned to make the best out of bad-boss situations:

- **Honor Leadership.** Part of my career plan is based on the premise to honor those in authority over me. This can be tough. Clearly, you should never turn a blind eye to unethical behaviors or abuse. I am solely referencing a difficult and disagreeable boss. Actively give honor to them. It may not change them, but it will change you.

- **Make your Boss Famous.** Another toughie. Why would you make a bad boss famous? Because if you can make them better, there's a chance your situation will improve. Don't talk up how wonderful your division outcomes are but give the glory for good things to your boss and take your lumps when things are not so good. Leadership demands humility. "There's no limit to the amount of good one can do as long has he doesn't care who gets the credit." Author unknown.

- **Take the Good.** Most bosses are bosses because they have done something good and have the capacity for more. Seek out the good and apply it to your career. My anti-whiteboard boss taught me the importance of having a "kitchen cabinet"— developing key informal relationships that serve as a sounding board and advisory committee. Life is too short to not learn from all circumstances.

- **Check the Mirror.** Take inventory of the bad and look for signs of these traits in yourself. If you find one, pull it out. Guard against bad boss behaviors creeping into your own style. If your boss is inclined to knee-jerk reactions, don't start flailing your arms every time you are faced with a challenge. Recognize bad boss behavior and never replicate it.

- **Leading Up**. This might seem impossible, but keep faith that you can influence a change in your boss. Lead by example. Although your voice may not be heard, your actions will be noticed, subconsciously or otherwise.

- **Think Long Term**. Look ahead and remind yourself that today's actions dictate tomorrow's decisions. If you quit when things are tough, you will become a quitter. Stick things out. Don't tap out too quickly.

- **Speak No Ill Will**. Avoid the trap of complaining about your bad boss to other people. This will only exasperate your situation and make it worse than it is. Speak blessings instead.

- **Seek First to Understand**. Figure out the drivers for bad boss behavior. They are likely stress induced. Most bad bosses are well-intentioned leaders who've lost their way because of personal and/or professional pressures. Identify the sources of stress and you might help reduce or eliminate it. At the very least, you will sympathize and realize the behavior is not a vendetta against you, albeit it feels like it.

- **Avoid a Bad Boss**. Forbes shares five tips for spotting a bad boss in an interview. Gather your own references. Call the person who most recently held the position. Call on the other direct reports. If you are well networked, get the internal buzz on your potential boss. Many a bad boss situations could be avoided if you researched diligently and listened to what you heard. Don't believe things will change because you believe you are better than your references. They won't.

- **Joy in Suffering**. This is the toughest one for me, but the most important. "Suffering produces perseverance; perseverance builds character; and character produces hope." It's an upward, spiraling cycle throughout life.

So if you have a bad boss, you have a choice. Life is too short to be in a bad boss situation but you owe it to yourself, your people, your boss, and your organization to make it work. I persevered with the anti-whiteboard boss. I established a "kitchen cabinet," as I'd learned from him. I was promoted out of that division and into corporate where I became CIO. Hope never disappointed me.

And I purchased the biggest damn whiteboard ever made.

MANAGE YOUR AURA

1997. The reverberating rave music generated a hip vibe. Cameras flashed as bright lights drew the crowd's attention to the student models. Attending my first fashion show, I sat at the end of the runway—as one of the judges. I felt like a punk rocker at a symphony. The dean of my alma mater had appointed me to the board of the fashion school (long story). My fellow judges—all of whom were in the business of fashion—and I were responsible for appraising the undergrad and graduate champions of design. Initially excited about the opportunity, I quickly realized my business skills didn't match up to my responsibility as fashion critic. (I hear your laughter. My daughter agrees.)

But I gained one valuable lesson through that experience. The beauty of a model or her/his clothing design didn't captivate me; the confidence with which the model walked did.

Lacking the typical, requisite seasoning for a CIO, I fell into the pose at a young age. My CEO asked me what I needed to be successful. "Two things," I replied. "A year of formal mentoring from you and a ticket to the CHIME CIO Boot Camp." I received both.

Although the Boot Camp curriculum and instructors proved incredible, time spent with my group leader, John Glaser, influenced me most. Here's one of the many pearls I received from him: "Learn to manage your aura or someone will manage it for you." I took his wisdom to heart.

Aura defined: "a distinctive and pervasive quality or character; air; atmosphere."

In the years since my Boot Camp graduation, I've aggressively assimilated this golden nugget. Borrowing from my friends in marketing, you have to *brand* or *be branded*. Here are a few ideas.

Network. Continually expand the breadth and depth of your professional and personal network. Proactively reaching out to others saves you from isolation and irrelevance.

- LinkedIn
- Twitter
- Facebook

Publish. Editors are interested in genuine stories from real leaders. Send queries and don't give up when initially rejected.

- Magazines
- Online services
- Blogging

Present. Get over your fears. Presenting forces you to nail your subject matter and confront fears.

- Professional societies
- Neighborhood associations
- Your organization
- Church, synagogue, etc.

Involvement. Jump into the community. Let leaders know you are interested in adding value.

- Professional societies
- Special interest groups

Volunteer. Find regular opportunities and your network will expand.

- Internally

- Externally

Routinely Self-Review. Schedule times to review progress and make adjustments. Ask for feedback.

- Update your brand
- Develop a career strategic plan
- Ask your mentor

Education. Take the initiative to self-educate. Learn from inside and outside of IT and healthcare.

- Blogosphere
- Marketing resources

Add to Existing Body of Knowledge. Comment on what others have to say. (You don't always have to be the author.)

- Post to blogs
- Contribute whenever the opportunity presents

No action will spoil your aura more than damaged credibility. So while I'm all about a personal hallmark, it must be built upon a solid foundation of execution. These are not sequential tasks. Proactively improve performance and brand simultaneously.

Keep your aura in perspective, and let this humble you. The value of a stellar aura should reach far beyond its owner, and its primary benefits should accrue to the people and the organization served. If not, then it's all about you. Possessing a personal brand—which should never come from arrogance or false humility—is key to success. For without it, you are allowing others to determine your brand.

You're on the runway, lights flashing, cameras clicking. Make no mistake; the crowd is analyzing your every step. So brand yourself and accentuate it with confidence.

CULTURALLY RELEVANT LEADERSHIP

One of my favorite things to do as a youth was to visit my dad's office. To get into the French Army compound unnoticed, I had to be smuggled, cloaked in an air of mystery and suspense. I'd hide under the dashboard of our military sedan as French security forces saluted our vehicle through the gate. Once inside, my dad would park the car in front of the U.S. Forces headquarters and, when given the clear signal, I would run inside where I savored a free existence among the U.S. military and civilian officials.

As my dad worked, I would pull up a chair to the massive wooden conference tables and desks and play office. I toyed with paper clips, erasers, pens, rubber stamps and other office paraphernalia. I loved using the electric typewriters and placing my classified papers into the filing cabinets that filled much of the hallway space. I made pretend phone calls to other consulates and raided whatever candy jars were available.

Fast forward...

In recent years, I have entered ex-IT leaders' offices to discover that not much had changed since my youth! Searching desk drawers, I was surprised to unearth rubber stamps, legal pads and stickers. (Remember those gold stars teachers used to put on report cards?) With the exception of computers, these offices were even equipped with yesterday's furniture. Although digital automation was functioning, you'd never know it by the amount of documents printed and processed via historical methods. Despite all the digital storage media available, I'd speculate that we still store more paper than ever before.

We have an aging leadership issue, and I'm not necessarily referring to chronological age.

Evidence supports the likelihood that our antiquated styles and methods are creating hindrances in raising the next generation of IT leaders. These future leaders need our wisdom, but are our succession plans hip enough to give us credibility? I am not the most avant-garde CIO out there, but I am cognizant of my need to continuously update my team and myself lest we become irrelevant to those whom we lead and serve. So I push myself. I still have a long way to go.

If I have offended you thus far, check your desk drawers.

Cultural relevance manifests itself in many ways: how we dress, lead, talk, use tools, interact with staff, innovate, etc. Assuming you already have the requisite IT skills, endeavor to keep up with cultural trends. What was relevant when you graduated is not so for today. Here is a test. Bring your father into your office. If he is comfortable with the tools you use on a regular basis, give yourself an "F!"

How to stay culturally current:

- **Hire and promote it.** Do not be afraid to hire new blood right out of school. Promote talented individuals even if they don't have years of experience. If they're talented, they're teachable.

- **Hang out with culturally current people.** Having had two teenagers in our home has acted as a catalyst for me. I have also created advisory groups to keep me on my toes. The best one was made up of second-year residents who gave me advice. I first learned of wikis and the power of blogs from them.

- **Experiment.** If you don't already have a LinkedIn and Facebook account, you are way behind. Bonus points if you conduct business via SecondLife.

- **Hang time.** Set up monthly after-work parties at the local watering hole, where people will be more likely to let down their guard and deepen relationships on a different level. You'll reap the benefits back at the office. I even had a foosball table in my office that helped eliminate intimidation and similar barriers.

- **Cross-pollinate.** Avoid spending your conference investments solely in health care. Attend non-healthcare venues and get to know people who don't look like you or share the same points of view.

- **Wardrobe.** Honestly, how old are your suits and ties? I picked the sharpest dresser in my IS shop and had him stop over to my house. He systematically eliminated about seventy-five percent of my work wardrobe. He then took me shopping -- and not where my dad shops.

- **Read voraciously.** Read blogs! Read from non-traditional sources of media. Gain fresh perspectives on everything from innovation to leadership. Managing Gen X requires different diplomacy than Gen Y, who require completely different techniques than do Baby Boomers.

- **Speak and write.** This process will force you to differentiate and expose yourself to new ideas, vocabulary and trends.

- **Reduce Email**. Email is from the 1990s. As my kids say, e-mail is for when you want to send a thank you to your friend's mom for having you over for dinner. Push the limits with IM, text messaging and video.

- **Furniture.** My office furniture has no place to store paper. There is no table, except for coffee. There is no trashcan. There is no printer. Everything (phone, projector, tablet) is wireless. We are tearing down several cubes in favor of contemporary design that encourages innovation and collaboration.

- **Music.** Hey, I love 1980s music. But I do my best to mix it up with the latest in sound. Listen to all—yes, all—that your employees listen to, from Mozart to Moby. Admittedly, I still struggle in Texas with country.

- **Phones.** Do you still have a flip phone?

Being culturally current cannot be delegated. Be proactive, otherwise you'll end up only attracting employees who like to stamp documents and store them in mammoth filing cabinets. Candy jars are acceptable.

THE NO NICE GUY RULE

I interviewed with University Hospitals on November 23, 1998. I recall the date for two reasons. One, it was my birthday. Second, I encountered Zoya (this is not her real name, I changed it to respect her privacy), an analyst on the employee interview panel. Zoya embossed herself on my memory with her questions. She pitched hardballs, fastballs, and curveballs while the nice people on the panel tossed softballs. Although professionally polite, Zoya hovered on borderline offensive. I was taken aback by her persona, yet her disruptive approach was about to make me a strong leader.

Let me explain.

My first day on the job, Zoya walked into my office and welcomed me. Before I could hang up my coat, she asked if I had time to talk. She was alive with ideas and energy and aspired to transform the IT culture and increase our value to our customers. Although overwhelmed at first, I appreciated her hunger to influence and shape our organization.

The customers loved this analyst. If no one kept watch, some customers would bypass our intake process and go directly to her. She tackled the most difficult assignments and notoriously challenged our processes. Zoya took great pride in consistently delivering results and delighting her customers. A workhorse! And…she was tough to manage.

While the customers loved Zoya, the IT team did not. One by one, each complained to me about her, and their observations had merit. I recall Zoya's first review. She gave herself a perfect score. In discussing career goals, she stated her expectation to be the best analyst in the world but agreed she hadn't reached that goal. Nevertheless, her drive to be the best showed in her outcomes, which inevitably raised the bar for the other analysts.

I invested in Zoya, an immigrant from Russia. She and her husband had packed up their kids one day and sought a better life in the United States. Sympathizing as a person of European descent, I coached her. I pointed her toward specific changes and how to better handle situations. I sent her to a speech pathologist to help her communicate more clearly. She made headway, slowly.

Still exasperated, the team now came into my office as a group to lay out their complaints. I listened and then asked: Who can tell me the names of Zoya's children? Silence. Who can tell me the names of her dogs, whose pictures she had plastered all over her cube? Silence. Who can tell me her passion (Russian folk dance)? Silence. Who can tell me her defining moment? Silence. Who can tell me her background and why she left Russia? Silence. Who can tell me what drives Zoya? Silence. "Once you're able to answer these questions, we'll revisit Zoya's future with us."

I endeavored to kill the notion that every instrument in the band had to be a clarinet. Collegial yes, but as long as behavior did not violate organizational values, every employee had the freedom to express themselves uniquely. Sure, it's cozy when the team can sing Kumbaya in harmony but who thrives under constant coziness? I'd rather work with a team of challenging personalities who add value to the business than a team who like one another but perform with mediocrity. I would argue that the conflicted team—dare I say disruptive and non-complacent—produces superior individual and team performance. Iron sharpens iron. Better to celebrate individual differences than succumb to the tragedy of nice guys. I want people and leaders who walk their own path, even if it's not nice.

The team never came back with another complaint. Instead, they engaged Zoya on a personal level. Mutual understanding and acceptance grew. They became a team. They gleaned from her, and although she never sang Kumbaya, Zoya did learn to be more collaborative and collegial. The team developed into a shining star for our IT division and launched me to where I am today. Thanks to Facebook, many of us remain connected after all these years.

Not all of my experiences with my teams have been positive. I've made mistakes. A couple of times I invested energy into helping a staffer turn the corner and be successful, but that person refused to change. Before you think I'm endorsing dirty players, let me balance my message. Consider the best seller The

No Asshole Rule by one of my favorite professors, Stanford's Robert I. Sutton. You have to protect your team. Get to know the fine line between a "not nice guy" and an asshole.

Yes, Zoya rocked our world but made us uncomfortable. Yet it didn't surprise me when our team rallied around her after she was diagnosed with stage-four cancer. We cried together over her death, for she had left a legacy in her own unique way.

Thanks Zoya, for not being nice, but for being true to yourself.

13

PHYSICAL FITNESS

fit • ness (fit'nis), n.
1. health. 2. capability of the body of distributing inhaled oxygen to muscle tissue during increased physical effort.

Fitness enables health. Health enables energy. Energy sustains us and helps us perform our best. Fitness improves our mind's ability to think and experience.

I would not be climbing mountains if I was not physically fit. I would not be a triathlete and competing internationally if I was not physically fit. I would not be able to get through airports as fast as I do if I was not physically fit.

You create opportunities when you are fit. You have more energy, you have more strength.

I went to a seminar once and the group running it had this concept of the corporate athlete. If you are an executive, you really are not unlike an athlete and you need to train to stay in shape physically, mentally, emotionally and spiritually. I agree with this 100 percent! I believe that you really need to be fit to have these extraordinary experiences.

Treat yourself like an athlete. Eat well. You don't have to be excessive or obsessive, but treat yourself well and take care of your body and mind. We do fresh fruit Mondays or Fresh Fruit Wednesdays at my workplace. People don't need to work out three hours a day like I do—I would never recommend that for anyone when it's not part of your vision. But you can take an hour a day or walk—become more active and you will feel better.

Taking a walk or working out for an hour gives you time to think and reflect, also part of being fit.

FIT LEADERSHIP

What to do? Our flight left Jackson Hole way behind schedule. Sitting next to me was a colleague from our cross-town rival. We both grew anxious about the possibility of missing our connecting flight out of Chicago. We landed late. We had twenty minutes to traverse O'Hare to catch the commuter to Cleveland Hopkins airport. Conference fatigue might have been a factor, but before we exited the jet bridge, evidence suggested that we were not going to make it to the departure gate. At least, *not together*.

As I write this, New Years is fast approaching. This is a traditional time for reflecting on the past and setting vision for the future. Crafting plans. I do this annual exercise for myself, my career, *and* with my family.

Need a new challenge?

Consider making the coming year a year of managing energy and getting fit. If you can't do this for yourself, then do it for others. The people and communities you serve and influence deserve the best you can give. Not to mention your family.

Energy is our most critical resource, yet most of us fail to manage it effectively. Year after year, leaders are asked to do more with less, be more productive, remain fully engaged. If our bodies are not trained to handle the stress load, then the demands on our energy will exceed our capacity. This state of poor health results in lower productivity, disengagement, unfulfilling relationships and compromised leadership.

I want to live a satisfying life. But am I willing to do what it takes to get there? Are the benefits worth my effort, my sacrifice? According to my wife's trainer, "You're never too old to see changes."

The resources are out there, so ignorance is no excuse. I like the American Heart Association's model and I urge everyone to take their short "The Simple 7" assessments. I was shocked to learn that less than one percent of the US population meets "The Simple 7" criteria. Retired generals and admirals recently sounded another alarm bell this year with their treatise on "Too Fat to Fight." Casual observation suggests healthcare leaders are not immune. How can we get to accountable care without first living it ourselves?

Ample evidence shows positive correlations between fitness and energy levels and performance and life satisfaction. The Human Performance Institute offers a course for the corporate athlete, one I recommend. In their holistic approach, which encompasses the physical, emotional, mental, and spiritual aspects of life, the Institute reported the following results amongst graduates:

- 75% report they are more engaged with life

- 62% report they are more engaged with their family

- 65% report they are more engaged in taking care of their health

- 48% report improvement in self-confidence

- 57% report they are more productive at work

- 42% report they get better sleep

- 61% report they are more likely to take positive action to make changes in their lives

Being fit provides other benefits. I worked for an organization that gave health insurance discounts based on compliance with one or more of their five measures of health. I worked to meet each criterion, and *my health insurance costs were zero!* If I want to keep up with my wife, I've got to be fit. She reminds me that someday we will have grandchildren, and she wants to be able to run and play with them. Heck no, I'm not going to be left sitting on the playground bench!

At family reunions, my nephews love to play soccer and touch football, and I'm determined not to be outdone…by too large a margin, anyway. I have significant interests outside of work, and I know I could not perform any of them well let alone attempt them without adequate energy management.

I had a choice to make that day in O'Hare. Stay with my colleague and watch our flight depart without us, or leave him behind. I decided that making it home to spend time with my family was more important than spending time with a rival. I moved along and made the flight just as they were closing the door. Yes, that is a silly story, but how many connections do we miss in life because a lack of energy? We've all missed personal and professional flights—and regretted it.

Make a resolution. Make the coming year The Year of the Fit Leader.

DO YOU HAVE WHAT IT TAKES?

Interestingly and not surprisingly, my most popular posts are not on healthcare or technology but on leadership. It seems that industry-specific challenges and solutions are secondary to the primal importance of leadership. You can have great ideas and vision, but if you lack leadership, well, as Robert De-Niro would say in one of his organized crime roles, "faahget about it".

We are born questioning life. A range of insecurities affects different individuals. Many search their entire lives for answers, and few find them. One question I often ask, "Do I have what it takes?"

Athletes wrestle with this question, especially before an event. During the Escape to Alcatraz competition vibrant energy flowed from the participants as the boat headed toward the island prison. We discussed race strategy, weather conditions, currents and the great deals we got on our technically advanced wetsuits. But as race time approached, an eerie silence took over. Some would say it was the sound of focus.

I'd argue it was the deafening throb of introspection. *Do I have what it takes?*

When I completed my first extreme adventure race, it was daunting: forty miles of technical mountain bike trails, thirteen miles of kayaking, one mile of river swimming and twenty miles of running, all integrated via traditional map and compass. Before the starter pistol fired, I listened to people sharing battle stories from the adventure race season. As the minutes wore down, I began to grasp the reality of my latest endeavor. No marked trails. My team would be on our own, finding our way with no support other than what we could carry. *Do I have what it takes?*

When I held my first child; when I first spoke in public; when I first led troops; when I took on my first CIO role and faced numerous challenges—I asked myself *the question*. I've tried to live in such a way that I can answer in the affirmative. I know that having what it takes revolves largely around preparation, which breeds confidence. And I'll tell you what, when you're floating two miles off shore between San Francisco and the frigid waters of the Pacific, you had better be able to answer positively!

Simply put, we don't rise to the occasion; we fall to the level of our preparation.

Where athletic pursuit boasts of physical demands, leadership carries the challenges of high stakes, decision-making, and time pressures, to name a few. We need to do everything within our control to prepare for whatever work might throw at us. Some things we can't prepare for. Life is full of surprises, disappointments and crises. Nevertheless, we must be ready for the ultimate question—and have the confidence to answer. If finding a solution requires a lifeline of some sort, coordinate that in advance. I know I need a lifeline, and my ultimate confidence is grounded in my faith. Combining faith with preparation enables me to ask and answer the question affirmatively. You many not require a lifeline or you may draw upon a different foundation, but one thing is for sure: you must be prepared to answer.

Whether my next challenge is at work or in the frigid waters of San Francisco, I will ask myself the question. And despite my fear, I will put my face into the waters and put one hand in front of the other and stroke. I have what it takes. Do you?

WORK-LIFE BALANCE...DEBUNKED!

The first thing we boys did after disembarking from the school bus was to head north to the neighborhood 7-Eleven. Liberated from a day of junior high classes and a numbing thirty-minute bus ride, we hungered for entertainment. Pinball was the rage then and we all sought the coveted crown of being best at The Who's "Pinball Wizard."

Grasping the corners of the machine, I'd let my fingers become one with the flipper-buttons, slapping the ball into the pins and rails and racking up points. In the heat of the moment, I'd jiggle and rattle the sloped table, eager to outscore my buddies. And then…it would happen. My overzealous manhandling would cause the dreaded *tilt*—the machine disengaged—and my silver ball drained straight down the middle. Even as I write this, I can hear and feel the ominous skull-pounding, buzz. I lacked the perfect touch between allowable manipulation and sheer force. *Tilt!*

We all go through life encountering a fair amount of *tilt*. The abundance of balls we're juggling crash to the floor because we can't manage them all. The contemporary word for the phenomena today is "balance." Bookstores carry dozens of books on the subject, and magazines print oodles of articles trying to help us live balanced lives and avoid a *tilt* scenario.

As CIOs, our careers are demanding and change is a common constant. Yet families are our support and our hobbies provide fulfillment and, thus, both deserve our time. We desire to perform well in all aspects of life. It's how we're wired.

I never experienced as much imbalance, or *tilt*, until I tried to seek the elusive balanced life. I'd read all the articles and believed the myth. Like the man chasing the end of the rainbow, I found a pot of disappointment instead of gold. In my stressed effort, I tried to run faster.

At last, it occurred to me. In this information age, the balanced life is not achievable. Nor should it be. We fool ourselves into thinking that life is made up of set components with solid boundaries that stack neatly together like Tetris, with micro interfaces where convenient.

I advocate a different approach—Life-Work Integration. We all look for ways in which to maximize areas of our lives without having a negative impact on our values and ideals. We all desire to live a life of significance. I had the privilege of speaking on this theory at a recent healthcare professional society meeting. The president had heard me touch on the subject a year back while giving a talk on mentoring; he thought the concepts would be of value to his society. Based on the session feedback, the ideas resonated with the majority of attendees.

Balance implies that you give up something on one side of a scale until both sides are even—an exchange. Integration, on the other hand, is fluid and dynamic, bending and blending endeavors—*time* sharing. I don't want to allocate fifty hours for work, ten hours for fitness, twenty-five hours for family, fifty hours for sleep, etc. I want to bend and blend—to work sixty hours one week but thirty the next. I want to symphonically synchronize the flow of all my roles and responsibilities. I may have a desire to get up early and complete an outstanding task, or catch all my daughter's daytime dance recitals. I may need an extra ten hours per week to perfect the Argentine Tango with my wife, made doable by combining practice with our weekly date night. I don't turn off my connectedness to any aspect of life. It is fluid and dynamic, bend and blend.

Here are some everyday examples of integration. One that serves me well is my virtual office. This setup untethers me, further enabling bend and blend opportunities. I carry a single device, and my digital schedule reflects all of my life roles, including my "honey do" list. No more home phone, multiple email addresses, or home PC to slow me down. I network socially through a *single* portal. Ninety-five percent of my athletic events have, in some aspect, included one or more family members. And I try to bring at least one family member on every business trip.

I leverage systems, as well. I belong to an athletic club offering multiple locations. Depending where I start my day, I find the nearest club, all of which are preprogrammed in my GPS. Then there are repetitive tasks. You can hard wire these so you have more time and energy to focus on things that will have greater impact. Andy Stanley states that "systems can have a greater impact on behavior than mission statements."

A strong foundation will enable life-work integration and help avoid *tilt*. Some key aspects:

- Develop and maintain a strategic plan for your life.
- Make sure principles/values are well defined and unmoving.
- Ensure your life passion is identified and calibrated.
- Surround yourself with accountable relationships and mentors.
- Embrace technology to master time and leverage efficiencies

(don't let them master you).

- Create margin and set boundaries.
- Develop systems to support your principles and plans.
- Expand your creative capacity.
- Adopt a consistent worldview and belief system (for me this is based on my faith).
- Man up and make tough choices.

The last one is the hardest. Many people go through the process of prioritizing and discovery but then fail in the execution because they won't pull the trigger on the difficult choices that would propel them to the next level. No one can do everything. Creating healthy boundaries often means eliminating the "good" in order to keep the "great." Yet, out of a fear of change, of hurting others, or other perceived pains, some continue down the same path, trying to find an unachievable balance.

Take some time to reflect on this post and the possibilities of life-work integration. Review the elements of a strong foundation and how they might keep you from Tilt.

You can do it!

CRISIS REVEALS LEADERSHIP

I finished my first week as CIO exhilarated. I slipped out early and headed for a haircut (I had hair back then). The grating *buzz* of the "emergency broadcast system" disrupted WTAM radio's sports update. A power outage that began in the Northeast had hit Ohio. This was not a test. Out the window, I watched traffic come to a halt. Electricity stopped, rendering traffic signals colorless. I called my family and staff but cell networks were overwhelmed. I returned to the office.

They say nothing in life is certain except death and taxes. I disagree. Crisis is a sure thing. By definition, *life* is a series of crises and showcases of our ability to react. Death, sickness, raising teenage daughters—life and career choices determines the amount and severity of crises you might experience. But one thing remains true, you will have them. Great leadership will minimize the volume of crisis, but every leader will encounter one. Preparation and execution determines how healthily you emerge.

No course, audit, or survey can tell you as much about your leadership than a crisis. If you want a test that shows what you are made of, crisis will reveal your abilities. Those who aspire to greater responsibility must understand that to whom much is given much is required. The higher your position, be it family, church, community or work, the higher the probability that you will be leading in crisis. Be prepared.

I have mishandled some crises and led well through others. In each case, I came to terms with my abilities. Failures and successes totaled, here are things I learned. Master these so they become part of your core leadership abilities.

Take Responsibility Immediately. Do not blame a vendor or an employee. You are the CIO, the leader. This crisis happened on your watch. Take responsibility and focus on resolution.

Leadership:

- **Chain of Command.** Ensure everyone knows chain of command, especially when multiple teams are involved in working on solutions. Establish sleep cycles, you do not want lack of clarity to slow progress.

- **Battlefield Promotions.** Expend your energy working with the motivated, not trying to motivate the worker. Make on the spot promotions as needed. Now is not the time for staff development.

- **Fit Leader.** Sometimes a crisis can span multiple days. You have to be fit to be effective. Don't argue with me, argue with science. Most can perform well for 24 hours, but notable performance degradation begins thereafter.

- **Visibility.** You must be on site. Make a point to lead all customer calls (except on sleep rotation) and walk the floors of impacted hospitals. Walking floors is mandatory for all the command center commanders (my direct reports).

- **Deploy Listening Posts.** During a crisis, it may appear that the sky is falling. You'll hear exaggerated reports. Your plans may be incongruent with reality and spread panic and fear. Having your own listening posts will help discern reality and lead to quicker resolution. This is another reason why personally walking the floors is critical.

- **Ask the Right Questions.** We live in an instant society with on-demand entertainment and microwave food. We often don't have all the pieces necessary to solve a problem that might arise. The delta between the immediate need for an answer and the time it takes to find the right solution frequently generates stress. In this scenario, stress begins to ebb when you finally start asking the right questions and start getting the right answers. And, like any good jigsaw puzzle, the pieces naturally begin to fit together... as they were intended to.

Processes:

- **Operations.** The operational process you choose to leverage is immaterial, but having established routine processes is a key factor for success when crises hit. You do not have time to reinvent the wheel.

- **Downtime Procedures.** Again, establish and practice.

- **Disaster Recovery/Business Continuity.** Most organizations have a DR plan, but few have BC drills. Conduct BC drills quarterly. This enables you and your staff to better handle the stress and drama of an actual crisis before it happens.

- **System Access.** Avoid single points of failure. In an emerging world of ubiquitous electronic health records, you must have devices and systems predeployed to ensure access to data in a catastrophe.

- **Business Resumption Plan.** While it is key to focus on solutions, you must also direct your staff and customers on business resumption planning well before the solution is in place.

Practical Logistics:

- **Food.** Assign someone to ensure a steady food and coffee supply. Let your key people focus on tasks, not noisy bellies.

- **Sleep.** Have a rotation for rest, like airline pilots on international flights. Have comfortable places for people to sleep and nap if staying on the premises.

- **Command Center.** Erect a center within one hour of calling a disaster and staff it 24/7. It should stay open twice the length of the actual event. Do not shut it down prematurely.

- **Assist Customers Impacted.**
  - Constantly ask, "How can we serve you? What else can we do?" whether IT-related or not. I deploy staff to deliver water supplies and purchase fans.
  - Double or triple the number of staff on site. Visibility during a crisis is crucial. Keep high staffing levels until the customer signals enough. I saw firsthand how our clinicians reacted to seeing a significant presence on the floors with questions like "How is the system working? How can I help?" This reassured our clinicians that we were taking the

crisis seriously.

- **Communications Plan.** Strong communication fills the void that otherwise gets populated with incorrect messages. It helps develop customers as allies in solving crises, as opposed to antagonists.

  - Publish your cell phone number.

  - Start all communications by highlighting your organization's mission. This serves as a common rally point for all involved.

  - Be consistent in your messaging. Key messages might include accountability, transparency, action, calm, and hope.

  - Execute your plan as published.

  - Leverage multiple venues such as conference calls, emails, collaboration tools, portals, etc.

  - Embrace corporate communications. They are experts in communications and can help you develop, adjust, and execute your communications plan.

Profit from Crisis.

- **Document throughout, and keep a history of all actions and issues.** This is critical in averting future crises. Resist the pressure to return an organization to status quo so you can profit from the crisis. Not seeking opportunities or pursuing the underlying cause of the crisis might leave your organization open for future conflict.

- **Wiki.** Open a wiki and encourage staff and customers to post notes in real time. Use these for practical insights during the crisis to document key lessons learned.

- **Document Lessons Learned.** Encourage all customers to take notes during the crisis so they can later make adjustments to the processes.

- **Downtime Procedures.** These may never have been exercised. The best time to make real world adjustments is while downtime procedures are active.

Engage Outside of IT

- **External Expertise.** It is a sign of strength to reach outside of your organization for help. If I sense the crisis is longer than two hours, I am on the phone calling peers and vendors.

- **Guru Council.** Set up a council of advisors to make sure your plans are logical and nothing is missing. Council members are not in the heat of the battle and can provide unstressed ideas.

- **Vendor Management.** Do not hesitate to escalate early and often. You have no time to dally. Let the level of severity determine when to go to the CEO.

- **Engage Senior Leadership.** Do not hide what is happening. Engage senior leadership immediately and keep them informed. Bring senior leadership directly into the loop with vendor senior management. This ensures your crisis will receive appropriate attention.

Internal

- **Take care of your staff.** Keep everyone focused on solutions not blame. Share all positive feedback as received.

- **Have multiple teams** working on multiple solutions. On two occasions, the primary plan failed to bring about resolution. Fortunately, secondary plans already underway saved the day.

- **Ask for ideas** from staff not associated with the crisis.

- **Levity.** Despite the crisis, you must work hard to ensure a calm atmosphere. Staff will think more clearly when you de-stress the environment. I recall day two of a crisis when someone began playing Christmas music and a sing-along started. It alleviated an otherwise tense situation.

Ending Well. When the crisis is over, the work begins. Send a thank you message and personally acknowledge all those impacted, first your customers and then your staff. These might include nurses, medical staff, and practices. Then figure out what happened and what can be done to avoid this same crisis. Do not skip this. Publish the results and include action and mitigation steps. Monitor for execution.

We are all healthcare IT leaders, and my hope is that some of you might profit from the ideas posted. What ideas and tips do you have that I failed to cover?

14
EXCELLENCE

ex • cel • lence (ek′sə ləns), n.
1. the fact or state of excelling; superiority, eminence:
his excellence in mathematics.

Whatever you do, you must do it with excellence, otherwise it's not worth doing.

When you perform all that you do with excellence, you not only have more pride in your accomplishments, but it sets an important tone for those around you and those who choose to follow you. Excellence breeds excellence and sets the table for above average experiences.

I was the line judge at a soccer match between Notre Dame and Air Force Academy at the Air Force Academy stadium, a big stadium full of Air Force Academy fans. There was a play where a ball grazed the back of an Air Force Academy player before going out of bounds. Everyone in the stadium thought the ball missed her and that it should be Air Force's ball. The player the ball hit and I were the only two people who knew the truth. I was tempted to go along with the crowd and let it be Air Force's ball. I knew that it would be hell if I called it the right way. All of this went through my mind in a split second. I made the call and gave the ball to Notre Dame and I was right: the crowd went wild with boos and yelling. It was brutal. Afterwards the player acknowledged that I had done the right thing.

Lesson: you have to do the right thing even when it's not popular. Always do the right thing, always strive for excellence.

FALLING FROM GRACE

If you've read my writings before, you know I practice transparency—perhaps to a fault. This chapter is the deepest view into my soul I have shared to date. I believe intense introspection is the way to exponential growth. Yet as I write my conscience fears what it will discover. The truth will come out.

I recently received an endearing card from my godson Josh that sparked this round of self-examination. I'll share excerpts first, and then I will answer him publicly because I believe it matters.

Uncle Ed,

Thank you for being such a great, if not the best example of a Christian...of a marriage...of a man...you motivate me and my brothers to be the best we can in athletics, faith and relationships...."

Dear Josh,

I received your thank you card yesterday. As your godfather, I am proud of you. First and foremost, you are a man of great character. You love God. You are accomplished. In high school, you worked diligently to attain Eagle Scout while earning the standing of class valedictorian. Your recent election as student body President pro Tempore at the University of Denver did not surprise me. All of this made the accolades you wrote about me so special, and they truly made my year! However, your extravagant praise and your interpretation of my external "face" have pushed me to reexamine my life from the inside. As a husband, father, executive, and (former) army officer, there are covenants and codes of conduct I have to put into practice. Combined, these rules and responsibilities have weighed heavily upon me....

Each week, the headlines highlight how so-and-so leader has fallen from grace. I am scared to be next. No leaders start out purposefully to do something that will land them in trouble. The politician never thought he would be sexting. The pastor did not go through seminary aspiring to have an adulterous affair. What executive ever dreamed of climbing the corporate ladder and becoming an alcoholic? The clinician didn't expect to take meds to quiet his own pain. No accountant ever thought to embezzle through sleight of numbers nor did any businessperson ever think she would entertain a bribe in exchange for wealth.

What is the trigger that leads a leader down this slippery path? I suspect it's a gradual slide, and if unchecked, this slide will get too steep to catch ourselves.

As our careers grow, natural protective barriers fall away. An increase in disposable income opens the door to more temptation. We come to expect perks. Rules no longer apply to us. Success can become a drug, and we begin to think, "I am invincible!" We take advantage of options that allow us to avoid accountability.

Success can become a vice in itself that creates an unquenchable thirst for more. We lose touch with reality in a gradual process that goes undetected. Before long, we're over confident and no longer count the costs of our indiscretion. We take our base for granted, assuming they will catch us when we fall.

...**So Josh,** my blessed godson, thanks for the reminder of why I need to live a life beyond reproach. To you and your brothers, I offer the following wisdom:

Shore up Home Base: Ensure your home life is solid; build a foundation strong enough to withstand the storms and temptations.

Engage a Counselor: Asking for help is a sign of strength, not weakness. The best ball players all have coaches.

Aggressively Secure an Accountability Partner: Find someone who will speak truth to you and not let you get away with crap—someone willing to put their friendship on the line if needed to keep you living right.

Live Humbly: Pride comes before a fall.

Spiritual: Let your faith be your source of strength, comfort, and significance. Seek purity of mind, body, and soul.

Embrace Fear: Healthy fear initiates boundaries. It's a great motivator. (I recently listened to Magic Johnson recount the story of confessing to his pregnant wife that he had AIDS. Heart wrenching. Don't do things you'll later regret.)

Live Transparently: No secret email addresses or phone numbers or bank accounts.

Set Boundaries: Don't mentor the opposite sex. Sounds draconian, but it protects both sides. Where appropriate, meet in public places or invite others to join you. Don't go to bars if you are prone to drink too much....

Reality Rocks: Ground yourself in reality. Shake yourself out of fantasy by mentally carrying out your actions to their logical conclusion. (Those who live fantasy lives will eventually get caught.)

Stay Strong: Some will find this advice offensive and poke fun. That is okay. I have watched lives get ruined, and I've cried with those who've fallen. Do whatever it takes to protect yourself.

To my leader friends: are you making progress that will prevent you from heading down the slippery slope to your own personal fall from grace? I am.

Tell someone. Get help. Cut the ties that are pulling you down.

Don't be next.

EXCELLENCE, THE ROAD LESS TRAVELLED.

Another summer working for meager wages was no longer an option for either my friend John or me. Both married with kids, we searched for a breakaway strategy where we could make decent cash to hold us over until our first big break. Under experienced and over educated in the utopic college town of Fort Collins, Colorado, our quest for adequate income proved a herculean task. Nevertheless, armed with respective degrees in psychology and Spanish (teaching certificate), we came up with a vision that would forever change our lives. We started our own company: **Men...Who Do Windows!**

We visited our local janitorial supply store. With ten minutes of in-store advice and a $100 investment in buckets, soap, and squeegees, we were bound for glory.

After analyzing our competition in the Yellow Pages, we realized we'd need a bold approach. Competing with dozens of vendors yet having no time or money for static advertisement, we took an unconventional approach. We created fluorescent colored flyers and paid teens to deliver them to targeted neighborhoods. Our phone began to ring.

We bid each job in person and dressed in nice clothes. We parked our "company car," a urine-colored Honda CVCC, down the road a few houses so as not to tarnish the high-end brand we strived for. Who would notice the 24-foot extension ladder strapped on top of an eight-foot car? We wore "uniforms." We priced our services higher than our competitors—a bold move. But we hoped to differentiate ourselves by stressing customer service and excellence. Included in our bid was our *happiness guarantee:* "We not only clean your windows but your screens and window sills as well. When we enter your home we take off our shoes. We have towels under all of our tools so you never need worry about us leaving your home a mess. We will move all drapes and curtains and furniture as needed.

All smiles after winning the 2013 CHIME/HIMSS John E. Gall CIO of the Year Award. Orlando, FL Feb 2014

Prior to us leaving your home, we will inspect each window with you. If you are dissatisfied with any we will redo them until you are happy with our work." We closed ninety percent of our bids. Our window redo rate? Less than one percent.

After a few weeks, we could not keep up with demand and had to stop all advertising. It became vogue in some neighborhoods to have a Men...*Who Do Windows* sign in the yard. A few customers insisted on serving us lunch on their decks overlooking a lake. Excellence creates demand.

We resurrected the business the following summer with the same results. We grossed an average of $400 per day with the cost of our labor-intensive business a low five percent. Excellence is profitable.

John and I believe our success was attributable to the high quality we put into our craft. We encouraged one another to be at our best as we honed our squeegee skills to ensure a streak-free finish. Why would people willingly pay a fifty-percent premium for our window-washing services? Because they knew it would be done to perfection. Our customers knew we would meet expectations and not leave without their approval. Excellence elevates the performance of those around you.

We both replicated this value in our personal and professional relationships—John as a teacher and later as a pastor, and I in healthcare. This pursuit of excellence blessed our families and careers. Moreover, the people and organizations we serve have benefitted. Excellence creates differentiation that separates good from great.

Ten years after Men....*Who Do Windows*, I was invited back to Colorado State University to serve on the advisory board of the college from which I received my master's degree. During lunch, I was approached by a fellow board member who asked if I had ever cleaned windows. I revealed myself as the founder of *Men*. He looked me straight in the eye and earnestly exclaimed, "My windows have never been so clean!" Imagine, ten years later and he still recalled the service he received from our company. Excellence is not forgotten.

Twenty years after Men....*Who Do Windows*, both John and I visited Ft. Collins with our families. The owners of Trios AVEDA Spa and Salon knew we were in town. They had a big social after-hours shindig taking place one evening, and yes, they asked if we could reprise Men....*Who Do Windows* and clean their windows so they would dazzle. We obliged. It was a great reunion and we still had our skills. Excellence sets a pattern for future performance.

The Men....*Who Do Windows* experience was a priceless time of formation. Alas, the time came for us to move into our chosen professions. Rather than sell the business, we gave it away to others in similar circumstances as we had been two years prior. We taught them everything we had learned, from window washing basics to customer relationship management and even the happiness guarantee. By the end of the first season the business lost half its value and we mourned when Men....*Who Do Windows* folded mid-way the following year. Excellence requires passion to attain and sustain.

A long time ago, a writer in Greece observed games that would eventually become the Olympics. He said, "Do you not know that in a race all the runners run, but only one gets the prize? Run in such a way as to get the prize. Everyone who competes in the games goes into strict training. They do it to get a crown that will not last, but we do it to get a crown that will last forever."

EXCELLENCE is doing everything you do with the very best you have.

THE LONG VIEW

I proposed to Julie on February 1, 1984. I was nineteen. I'm not sure I really knew what love meant, but I sure enjoyed being around her. I loved listening to her practice piano for recitals and stealing second glances. Despite our young age, everyone was pretty stoked about our engagement, except her parents. Looking back 27+ years later, with my own daughter that age, I can't really blame them.

Julie defined their marriage. She was the apple of their eye. They wanted to delay giving her away for as long as they could. And when they did, they hoped for a doctor or lawyer. At least those were the types they had over to dinner so Julie could meet them on weekends when she was home from college.

I recall pulling into their driveway one Friday. My Chevy Vega with the duct-taped hood cowered next to their lacquered Mercedes. Wearing baggy sweats and tennis shoes with holes, I was the definition of poor. While I grunted away in the Army Reserve as a private, her dad stood tall as a retired WWII naval officer.

They were against the marriage from the get-go and withheld their support. Then came the final meeting—one last chance to talk us youngsters out of a commitment that had failed them both previously. They hired an investigator who reported everything about me from teenage indiscretions to bank withdrawals to employment history. There was nothing new to Julie and out of exasperation came the final plea.

They offered me a handsome amount of money to walk away! This was the bribe I have alluded to previously.

I did not hesitate. I'd already counted the cost, and despite the fast and easy reward, I took the long view. I'd never had that kind of cash, but I knew money wouldn't make me happy. I said no. They walked away.

We face many temptations in our careers. Most are not so stark, but others manifest themselves in many forms. We all know of colleagues who took bribes from vendors to influence purchasing decisions. Eventually they got caught and lost their careers and reputations. The short-term gain never pays long-term dividends.

Reviewing hundreds of résumés over the years taught me to spot trends where applicants constantly jumped from job to job, each time trying to bank a modest increase. Although a person might receive payola by making so many moves in a short period, they likely won't land the big one. Who would hire someone whose trend says he might leave in a year? At some point, all the jumping catches up to you, especially at the highest levels. Think tortoise and the hare.

I do believe there are times you must *go to grow*. Other times you need to grind through challenges so your character can form and your leadership skills can blossom. I see too many people run at the first sight of trouble. Boy, I've been tempted myself. I recall one year a while back showing up at a new employer where it was clear I was way in over my head. Way over. Everyone was nice and it was a stellar advancement opportunity, but my insecurities got the best of me. After a few months, I humbled myself and called my former employer, asking to return. The COO, who had previously served as my mentor, said no. He explained that I needed to stick it out, learn, ask for help, adjust and succeed. As much as he wanted me back, he knew if I went in reverse, I would never reach my ultimate goal of becoming a CIO. I followed his counsel, and today I am living my career dream. Had I taken the short view, I would likely still be working in the same position today.

My in-laws ultimately had a change of heart and helped us with the wedding expenses. I appreciated the fact they wanted to protect their daughter from making such a huge commitment at a young age, not yet even a junior in college. I would've handled this differently, but again, I understood the motivation. We got married and worked our butts off to get through school and start our family. Today we are richly blessed, having taken the long view.

Whenever challenges hit me, I'm tempted by the short view. But one look at my family and my career reinforces the lesson. The long view pays off.

TRAINS

I spent my early years in Europe where travel by train was the most efficient form of transportation. I loved the excursions where we bypassed the autobahn, moving swiftly across the landscape of Germany and surrounding countries. Returning often as an adult, I became increasingly aware of the differences in how trains were run by country. Even my kids quickly learned that German and Swiss trains were always on time, while the French were often delayed or just plain cancelled. We crossed our fingers whenever we had to jump a train for France. I asked some Swiss operators why the French trains had such a dismal reputation, and they blamed it on the culture, that their processes were not as sharp as other countries.

In December 2010 I had a rude awakening that my internal operations—my "trains"—were more French than they were German. I realized that our culture, unattended, had drifted and that we had no logical processes that were detailed except in the minds of one or two key individuals. Not good. Around 2 a.m. on that fateful morning, one of my team convinced me it was time for a major change and that we needed *über* focus on process. Convince me… nothing! I was desperate!

Since then, I've learned that the majority of IT organizations across all industries don't have formal process plans. Based on historical success or experience, they operate without intention. Some do extremely well with this non-method, others don't. We operated well without a plan for years. But given the complexity of our increasingly digital healthcare world, the risk became too great to operate whimsically. We chose the ITIL (Information Technology Infrastructure Library) framework. I'm not endorsing ITIL, but it is the framework we selected for IT service management. As a result, we've seen significant improvements in our operations. And like most frameworks, ITIL isn't just about operations, but operations is the area we chose to focus on initially.

We started with a gap assessment. Yep, we had holes in our processes, and we knew it. Our train tracks were not always true. We started to close those gaps, reassess, find more holes, and filled them. We were tenacious. It became one of our top priorities. Three years later, we won the Pink Elephant Award, a major industry recognition of the impact of our ITIL journey. Again, it is just an external validation of what was taking place internally: a complete transformation of our operations. This train is going places, reliably!

If you find yourself with operations that are more akin to the French trains than the Germans, here are some steps you can take to transform your operations:

- Lead the transformation process personally so everyone knows how important this initiative is.

- Hire someone, redirect a current position if you must, so someone is focused one-hundred percent on your framework.

- Have an external review of all IT service management processes.

- Pick highest risk areas and focus relentlessly.

- Require IT service management certification as a condition of employment (I was in the first class).

- Require advanced certification of all your leadership.

- Make classes mandatory, and include administrative support.

- As momentum grows, add staff as needed to enable transformation, even if it means repurposing existing staff.

- Make your maturity level goals part of your key performance indicators to ensure everyone has skin in the game.

- Invest in an appropriate number of staff to become experts.

- Annual external assessments to review progress to KPI (Key Performance Indicators).

- Never lose the focus or determination, talk about it often.

Not everyone will be onboard. You will experience pushback from your own team. That is part of leadership. Have the vision and execute. Listen to your team and adjust accordingly, but never lose sight of the need to drive this until IT service management is fully integrated into your culture and folklore. An example of how this translates into transformation is that our rate of unplanned changes (emergency and urgent) has been reduced by more than forty percent.

But the best part is how our new focus on running our trains efficiently and effectively has impacted business and clinical performance. I am unable to share our metrics at this point, but the reason we won the Pink Elephant Award had everything to do with ensuring the reliability of our systems to enable superior business and clinical outcomes. Simply put, we save lives.

Perhaps your trains run well and IT service management is not an issue for your organization. Bravo. I know this was not the case for us. Today our customers can trust that our trains won't be delayed or cancelled. All aboard....

CAUTION! TEAMBUILDING AHEAD

My affection for teambuilding was sparked during the journey through Cub Scouts and Webelos. My Army experiences further taught me that survival depended upon team. We had to work as a unit to navigate our way through a forest or through complex situations while under fire. Eventually, I recognized the transferable benefits to the corporate world. Today, few things thrill me more than getting my team outdoors to test and build our collective capabilities.

Of course…there is an element of danger involved in these pursuits.

The Burn. My first civilian ropes course. I was a Director at Parkview Medical Center, and all leaders were required to attend this training. We had a blast pushing the boundaries. That is, until we got to the capstone element: the Power Pole. *"One participant climbs to the top of a utility pole using staples. Upon reaching the top, the participant leaps from the pole and attempts to catch the trapeze bar suspended in the air."*

A 45-foot pole towered above me. Few attempted to even reach the top, and I couldn't blame them. I was the last to go, and peer pressure and pride kept me from bailing out. I climbed to the highest point, and I still recall the effort it took to reach above the climbing staples and hook up to the safety line. Then I stood on top of the 12-inch wide utility pole. It swayed with the wind, keeping me off balance. About 10 feet out and two feet lower than my line of sight, the trapeze bar beckoned. I'd never felt so scared in my life—except the time I got arrested for joyriding when I was 14.

My halfhearted plan was to make it look like a strong attempt for the trapeze then just fall and wait for the safety line to catch. I removed my gloves, crouched, and made the leap. Before the safety caught, I grabbed the climbing rope attached to the trapeze. Gravity sucked me down about 10 feet until the safety jerked me into a halt. I hung in pain. The skin on the insides of both hands had ripped away.

Once I was lowered, the CNO and Emergency Department Director took me straight to the hospital. More agonizing than the burn was when the ED doc cleansed the wound before working on it. Even writing this makes me want to clasp my hands shut as I had done after the injury.

Lessons Learned:

- Never do anything half assed or *expecting* to fail

- When handling ropes, wear gloves!

Rapids. My team had accomplished the incredible. Over eighteen months as part of a start-up, they installed a new application across 23 disparate and independent-minded academic departments representing 750 physicians plus residents. To celebrate, they chose the teambuilding activity of river rafting. A month later, we entered the Class III/IV rapids of the Youghiogheny River. Although I rafted a bit in simulated beach assaults with the Army, I had zero experience with rapids. I became raft captain by default.

We hit the first Class II rapids (easy), and I fell out. My raft-mates grabbed for me, but the current was too swift. Floating downstream and getting beat up by underwater boulders I then remembered the training: float feet first and on top of the water. Easier said than done. The rafting company had a three-tier safety layer in place in the event a bozo like me fell out. Tier one failed. I was headed straight for serious Class III and IV rapids. A tier two guide in a kayak couldn't reach me. I started to panic, which made matters worse. In the distance, the tier three guide stood on a large boulder in the middle of the river with a rope. She threw out the safety line, and my eyes affixed like laser beams on my last hope. She couldn't have been more than 100 pounds, but she was all I had between life and death.

I grabbed the rope as I hit the Class IV rapids. A "keeper hydraulic" took me under. The jet-like flow ripped through every crevice of my life vest and helmet until I felt as if the water would strip away all my safety gear. The current pushed me under, and I fought for air. I saw the proverbial flash of my life. That one-hundred-pound saint on top of the boulder, to her credit, remained steadfast and eventually pulled me into an eddy. I stood there, shaking. The tier two kayak made its way toward me, and the sliver of courage I had left got me back in the water and reunited with my team. And yes, this entire event was caught on video thanks to the "package" we purchased from the tour group.

Lesson learned:

- Listen to and consider all safety precautions.

- Don't stick your ass out too far unless you're willing to accept risk (that's how I fell out of the raft).

- If you fall, muster your courage and soldier on.

Slide for Life. Prior to being commissioned as an Army Officer, all cadets had to acquire a RECONDO (for RECONaissance and CommanDO) certification. One of the activities in the course was the Slide for Life. You slide down a zip line across a lake, keeping your eye on the flagman on the far side. When the red flag is raised, you extend your legs straight until your frame forms an L-shape. When the flag lowers, you let go of the zip line and drop into the water. Given the trajectory, this posture enables you to hit the water butt first and the world is good.

With great amusement, I lingered after completing this event to watch the other platoons execute. Most did fine, but every once in a while, someone decided against the L-shape and let go in an I-shape. The soldier hit boots first resulting in spectacular somersaults. In other cases, some were too scared to release at all and ended up crashing into the sandbags at the end of the zip line.

Lesson learned:

- Follow instructions.

- Fear causes paralysis.

After a string of these traumatic experiences, I chose safer team building activities. Here's what happened:

Curling. One of my direct reports was a curling fanatic, so I agreed to some ice time. What could possible go wrong? We dressed warm and headed for the Mayfield Curling Club. My CTO was tall and aggressive. We were in this to win. I shoved our stone down the ice where he was sweeping to heat up the ice and influence trajectory. He pushed too hard on the broom and his feet came out from under him. He fell face first. When we rolled him over, blood gushed from his mouth where his teeth had punctured a hole through his lower lip. Our CMIO and two nurses applied first aid. Given the severity of the cut and apparent concussion, we called an ambulance.

I could just hear my CEO. "We lost our CTO to what? Curling?" Thankfully, the man was released the next day following observation and stitches.

Lessons Learned:

- Ice is slick as hell.

- Don't make fun of curlers.

The "low key" retreat. I held an offsite retreat once with no outdoor events. One of our team accidentally slipped and fell and messed up his knee before the meeting even began. A great object lesson in teamwork followed: The CMIO did an evaluation. The combat medic rounded up some gauze and wrapped the knee. The CTO ensured the meeting room was set up to accommodate the wounded. The non-clinicians fetched ice and painkillers. And, in an ultimate display of team, and because he knew nothing was broken, the injured team member refused to seek medical attention until after the day was done.

Lessons learned:

- Injuries can happen in any environment.

- It is smart to have clinicians as your direct reports!

Despite the potential for injury, if you haven't escaped with your team to develop relationships and strengthen the bonds, then plan one today. Hmm… perhaps climbing mountains should be avoided….

"OTHER DUTIES AS ASSIGNED"

Generally, in my writing here I try to give a transparent window into the life of a healthcare CIO. Certain aspects of being a CIO, which generally apply to the entire C-Suite, are the numerous *external* "other duties as assigned." The list is by no means complete and only reflects what I've grown to understand from working at two large healthcare systems. But I suspect every CIO operates in one if not most of these assignments. (I will remain purposefully vague as to which role is current or former.)

Politics. Be involved. Get out there and shake hands to further the cause of healthcare and your institution. Sometimes this means attending fundraisers for a politician who advocates for healthcare or for your city or state hospital association. Take part in advocacy efforts and help educate our governing bodies.

Fundraising. Lead by example through the opportunities that come your way. Create margin in the household budget. In addition to established opportunities, we created our own annual IT fundraiser for a children's hospital that raised over $100,000 this last year.

Parties. Important social gatherings pop up often, and attendance is not always voluntary. I started out naïvely; now I own a tux.

Appointments. Consider these an honor and an opportunity to give back to the larger community. I have held very formal state-level appointments as well as less formal city and county appointments on behalf of my employer. But don't be a wallflower. Speak up, invest yourself to further the cause. Otherwise, don't bother accepting the position.

Boards. Many organizations are in dire need of talented people to help provide direction and ensure accountability. These boards can range from overseeing an international for-profit corporation to providing guidance to a local, not-for-profit homeless shelter. Always check for potential conflicts of interest first.

Task Forces. Often times these are directly related to healthcare but in a broader community sense.

Advisory Councils. My all-time favorite was serving on the College of Design and Merchandising (fashion) Council at Colorado State University. I was the only non-model, non-designer asked to join the judging panel at the annual fashion show. Lights, models, cameras, crowds—and me sitting at the runway's end with a tie that didn't match my suit.

Professional Associations. It's critical to remain actively involved to advance our profession. I have served on several national HIMSS committees and as State Chapter President (Tennessee and Ohio). I have spoken on behalf of HIMSS and CHIME throughout the country.

Speaking and Publishing. There is a healthy expectation that we add to the body of knowledge by sharing best practices, evaluated experiences, and tangible results. I have spoken on behalf of and been published in and outside of healthcare. The bonus: it contributes to your growth.

The common thread between these "other duties as assigned" is what makes them so valuable and important and why you need to take an active role. They:

- Allow you to give back to the broader community at large

- Provide a framework for you to help advance a specific organization or initiative

- Enhance your own personal and professional development

- Broaden your networking and social contacts

- Enhance your organizations position in the community and profession

- Force you to think outside of yourself

- Ideally makes the world a better place

Strive for excellence in every way you can! By stepping outside your office and embracing these "other duties as assigned" you may not only find fulfillment but also unforeseen opportunity!

DATA-DRIVEN PERFORMANCE

I have a confession to make. While I am an über advocate of data-driven performance in healthcare and IT operations, I seldom apply these tools to my personal life. Sure, I look at data when I consider investments and major purchases, but, let me put it this way: *you'll never see me with a Fitbit!*

I am witness to the power of data to shape clinical transformation. Are you kidding me? Serving in organizations with mature electronic health records and advanced business intelligence tools, I see the evidence in our quality reports all the time. Bam! Data-driven outcomes for sure. Evidence-based medicine—

check. Ditto on the business side. In fact, my organization was among the first in the country to post our data-driven metrics online. Transparency is a great motivator.

For all my talk on leadership, innovation, connected health and business intelligence, you might expect me to be a walking wearable. Nope. I'm wired as a visionary and details are not my forte. I might have a grand idea for a party, but I leave the planning and execution to the detailed-minded organizers.

When it comes to athletic endeavors, I'm about getting to the finish line fast. Forget style and quality form—just get out of my path. Over the years, the downside of this method caught up with me as time was no longer my friend. Another confession: my performance had stayed flat for a few years. I wanted to see improvements, so I needed to change.

My friend Ben Levine is a perennial "top doc." He runs the Institute for Exercise and Environmental Medicine and is one of the world-renowned types who has been kind enough over the years to help train my mountain climbing teams. Ben took me through the paces of his research lab, and part of our deal meant I had to be in a study and sport a wearable for a while. After analyzing all the tests, he told me my body was capable of greater performance. My lifelong conditioning gave me a good base, including a resting heart rate of 40 (occasionally 6 BPM when asleep). But I had not reached my physiological potential.

I researched and found a triathlon coach to help me get to the next level of performance. Of course, it turned out to be Amari of Dallas-based Playtri, who is a total data hog. She stretches me (no pun intended) beyond my comfort zone with all manner of wearables and resulting analytics. In the past, I would cycle in a race and hope for the best by just doing whatever felt good. Now she had me monitoring a combo of heart rate, cadence, and wattage. Speed is secondary. If I focus on the analytics, the outcome (speed) will take care of itself. If I only look at speed, as I did in the past, I might dismount my bike only to find I have no legs left for the run and then bonk.

I posted last fall about qualifying for regionals and then for the national Duathlon (run/bike/run) championships. Through grit, I lucked out and secured the last spot (age group) on Team USA. It was not pretty, but I made the team. With the World Championship on the horizon as well as other pending important races, the time for data driven performance had arrived. It was a real life experiment—with me as the subject.

Time to walk the talk.

Albeit imperfect in my utilization, Amari's training formula is completely driven by near real-time data feeds. She makes adjustments based on daily training and race results. I dutifully wear the gear and upload. She parses the data, does meta- and microanalysis, and off we go.

So what were the 120-day results?

I am writing this post on the plane home from the World Championships in Pontevedra, Spain. I followed Amari's race plan, which was all data points. 150-165 BPM heart rate on the first 10K, 270 watts on the bike, never going lower than 165. It was not "outrun the person in front of me," but to be patient and focus on my data, and then the results would be my friend.

I finished in the top 25. I was the #4 American (an upgrade from #18 last fall) to cross the finish line. Data-driven performance! I'm a believer. I can't wait until I perfect the technology and discipline myself further under Amari's coaching to see even stronger outcomes. Personal life imitates professional.

We must all push our organizations and ourselves to become data driven.

While being data-driven leads to improved outcomes, no data tool could ever create the dramatic finish to the race in Spain. Intrinsic motivation does serve a purpose.

It was the home stretch with half a klick to go. I saw the Team USA Manager exhorting us to finish strong. Tim handed me Old Glory as I ran by and said, "Catch two more racers!" I caught my two as I turned into the stadium sprinting to the finish, waving my country's flag. Hearing chants of "USA USA USA." Tears of joy.

Go Team USA!

CHASING MERCURY... LEADING WITH EXCELLENCE

Each year, I participate in a couple dozen races. Everything from 5K runs to complex endeavors like Ironman, Spartan Beast or Escape from Alcatraz. I train like I race, like I work, and like I live—purposeful, intending to win.

I don't like losing. Although I enter races knowing my podium chances are slim, I still race to win. I push as hard as I can. What hurts more than losing is missing the podium by one athlete. Fourth place finishes kill me. I can recall every race where I lost because I gave up the will to win or I compromised my performance.

Heading into a Thanksgiving Day half-marathon, I wasn't about to accept another fourth place finish. As we assembled at the starting line, I saw a man with the wings of Mercury tattooed on his ankles. I figured if I followed on his heels, I'd have a chance for the podium. I chased Mercury for much of the race.

During athletic events, my body talks—loudly. A fast heartbeat. Strenuous breaths. Muscles strain. Then my mind tries to take over by making up appealing excuses. If I heeded my body's instinctive impulses, I'd stop. I'd hop on the couch, turn on Netflix, and throw down a beer. Of course, I don't stop. Then my mind tries to justify the very behavior I loathe. I tell myself to slow down, or walk. Worse, I become delusional and begin to believe that the lead I built early in the race has given me the right to go on cruise control. Why push harder if I'm already ahead? Does it really matter as long as I finish? Nobody else is working hard, and they are doing just fine. Who would know?

This same digressive situation manifests in the workplace.

Come on, we all wonder how those leaders we consider inept got into their positions in the first place. The Peter Principle explains some of it, but not all. So what happened to the others? You have to figure they performed with excellence at one time, but then something changed. Did the energy and passion drain? Perhaps they lost focus. How did the clarity that once existed vanish?

Somewhere along the trail, rationalization allowed intolerable excuses to excuse tolerable performance. Many leaders finish the race, but few do so with excellence. I fear embracing the fourth-place mindset in my work.

At Mile 5, with the wings of Mercury in sight, I felt strong. But my body was already trash-talking me. I ignored the impulses to slow down and stayed focused. At the turnaround point, I could tell I was in the top six, but I had the chase group on my heels. I thought about all those fourth-place finishes and what it would take to stay in the lead pack. I resolved to win. I shunned the mind games and pushed towards the finish. In the last two miles, a few passed me, but I still saw Mercury. I set a personal record for the half-marathon and finished first in my age group.

True leaders don't give in to complacency or entitlement, no matter their age, status, or tenure. Yesterday's performance made you the CIO, but it won't make you a podium finisher without an unrelenting resolve to win. Leaders push for the gold, bringing out the best in themselves and in others.

Chase Mercury.

15
CLOSING
WORDS

My hope is that throughout the reading of these stories, you took time to contemplate how to apply these principles to your daily life. Your tales won't look like mine, so don't aim for an identical outcome. And for Pete's sake, don't let me hear you say, "Wow, Ed you are living my dream," or "Those are some amazing stories," or worse, "Ed, you are one lucky guy." May that no longer be!

Be inspired! Remember, genetics, intellect, and background are NOT pre-requisites for your own tales. Success will follow when you adopt these principles holistically and truly living in the moment. Live life out loud in every aspect. Embrace life personally and professionally and, over time, you too will begin to experience extraordinary tales. Don't be surprised if others come to *you* and say, "You are living my dream."

Once you've begun your journey, email me at ed@edmarx.guru and share your tale. I know you will amaze me.